If Standing Together Is So Great, Why Do We Keep Falling Apart?

Tom Kraeuter

Emerald Books

P.O. Box 635
Lynnwood, Washington 98046

Training Resources • Hillsboro, Missouri

If Standing Together is So Great, Why Do We Keep Falling Apart?

Real Answers to Walking in Unity

©1994 Training Resources, Inc.

>8929 Old LeMay Ferry Road

>Hillsboro, MO 63050

>(314) 789-4522

ISBN 1-883002-13-3

Dedication

I humbly dedicate this book to Nick Ittzes, my pastor and my friend. Nick, I have learned more about God and His Word from you than any other human being. Thanks for your unwavering stance to do things by the Book. The reality of seeing you live your convictions has had more impact on me than you will ever know. Thanks for your patience, your love, your respect and your encouragement.

Thanks to

- *The congregation of Christian Outreach Church for so often demonstrating the principles I am sharing in this book.*

- *Those I have encountered over the years who have done the opposite of these principles. I have frequently been driven to the Word of God through heartaches and poor examples to find the right way.*

- *Jerry Waggoner who, unbeknownst to him, offered much inspiration for this book. Thanks for your caring heart, Jerry.*

- *Jennifer Brody, my editor. Jenn, this is the third book you have edited for me, and I have learned much about proper writing from you. Maybe someday I'll be able to do this stuff without you... but I doubt it. Thanks!*

- *Diane Lopez for time-consuming, careful proofreading. Thanks for finding my misstayks.*

Special thanks to Barbara, my wife, for constant encouragement, faithful support and undying loyalty. Barb, you're the best!

"If you have any encouragement from being united with Christ, if any comfort from His love, if any fellowship with the Spirit, if any tenderness and compassion, then make my joy complete by *being like-minded, having the same love, being one in spirit and purpose.*"

(Philippians 2:1-2)

Table of Contents

Introduction

Unity. Our clergy preach about it; Paul continually wrote about it; Jesus prayed for it. Unity means loving, caring and dying to self. It brings strong friendships, respect and strength for the Church.

My goal in writing this book is to help restore some of the power the Church has missed by neglecting to walk in unity. There is strength in walking together with our brothers and sisters.

Throughout this book I will offer not only a vision for unity but numerous ideas of how to practically walk together in love. Understanding the necessity of walking in unity with our brothers and sisters is only the beginning. When I was in seminary one of the professors consistently made a statement that became ingrained in all of us: "Don't just tell people what to do. Tell them how to do it."

Once we understand that unity is essential we also need to know how to do it. Going from grasping a truth to actually living it is something we humans often find difficult. We can give mental assent to an idea, but making that idea reality within our lives is much more challenging. Therefore much of this book is specifically geared toward helping us to walk in the unity the Lord desires us to have. I will endeavor to offer practical, Scriptural, proven ideas that can make walking in unity a reality.

If you truly desire to learn to walk in unity, I would suggest reading through the entire book once. After that go back and reread one chapter at a time and prayerfully consider what God would have you do in response to what you just read.

This book is not meant to be a comprehensive theological treatise on the concept of unity. Instead, it is intended to be a simple, practical handbook that any Christian can read to be encouraged and challenged in their pursuit of unity.

This book is not meant to be all-inclusive either. There are quite probably numerous ideas about walking in unity that I have overlooked. The principles contained herein are simply concepts I have learned over the years that I think can be beneficial to others.

My prayer is that this book will help the Church today become like the early Christians described in Acts 4:32 — "All the believers were one in heart and mind..." ❖

Chapter 1

Virtual Reality

Virtual reality. It's an amazing new tool that can allow someone to learn to fly an airplane without ever even getting into a plane. It can give tours of houses to prospective home buyers without ever leaving the office of the real estate agent. It can offer the thrill of an automobile race or the excitement of a sword fight by simply visiting a nearby arcade. And much, much more.

Recently someone mentioned to me the possibility of creating a virtual reality church. The building, the decor, the pastor, the worship leader, singers, instrumentalists, choir, even the congregational members could all be stored on a C.D. ROM disk on a computer. Then you could make your own decisions every time you decide to "go" to church. Your personal preferences would dictate the style of architecture and surroundings. You could choose a pastor (or several); virtually any pastor in the world could be accessible. You would be able to pick your own worship leader. The instruments being played, the harmonies being sung, the style(s) of music, even the songs used would all be your choice. You would even get to determine who you would like to have at church that day. You could pick the people you really like, or, more importantly, leave out the ones you dislike.

The beauty of this whole concept is that you get to make all of the decisions and no one else can mess things up for you. No worries about whether the message for the day might be too close to home for your comfort; you choose the topic and even the style of delivery. You would never need to sing songs with which you are unfamiliar or uncomfortable; you pick the songs. Even the volume of the music is yours to control; make it as loud or as quiet as you want. Best of all you never have to be concerned about relating to people who make you uneasy. No bothersome relationships in the virtual reality church — only the folks you can really understand and relate to.

The whole concept is so perfect I am thinking about patenting it. If for no other reason, patenting it might keep anyone from actually doing it. You see, relationships and learning to work through our differences is a big part of the Kingdom of God.

After salvation, the thing that Jesus spoke of the most when He was physically here on earth was walking in unity. We need to understand that our relationships with each other, even with those we do not fully understand or relate to, are vital.

Let's Ask Peter, "What is Really Important?"

Suppose for a moment that you had the opportunity to meet the apostle Peter. If you were to ask him what he thought was the most important thing for us to learn about the Kingdom of God, how do think he would respond? What would Peter — the man whose shadow touched people and they were healed, the man who walked closely with our Lord Jesus for three years — what would he say should be our top priority?

In his first epistle, mainly a letter of encouragement and admonition, Peter tells us very clearly what he believes is most significant for us. He says, "*Above all*, love each other deeply..." (1 Peter 4:8). These are strong words. Nearly every translation I checked used the words "above all." This is not just a side issue. Additionally, instead of "deeply" some translations used "fervently" or "intensely." This obviously is not meant to be a half-hearted action.

Of course, in making this statement Peter is assuming that our relationship with the Lord is strong. However, his words echo the words of Jesus.

One day the Pharisees asked Jesus, "What is the greatest commandment?" He responded, "'Love the Lord your God with all your heart and with all your soul and with all your mind.' This is the first and greatest commandment. And the second is like it: 'Love your neighbor as yourself'"

(Matthew 22:37-39).

Most of us understand the first one. Loving God with all our heart is a given. To us this is a foundation in our walk with the Lord. However, that second part is often a bit more difficult for us. Loving imperfect people is always more challenging than loving a perfect God. People have flaws. People have opinions that differ from ours. People fail us. Loving them can be difficult.

The fact of the matter is that unless you close up shop and try the virtual reality church you will always have to deal with people. And, unfortunately, people will often hurt you, mistreat you, and sometimes point out things in your life that really do need to change. How will you respond? Will you endeavor to be humble and gentle, considering others better than yourself? Or will you run to try out virtual reality?

Not Always the Easy Road

There are times that I feel it would be much easier for me to run. However, more and more I am realizing that one of my very highest priorities is to intensely love my brothers and sisters in Christ. This means walking through and working through our differences. It means not running away from difficult encounters but facing them head on.

It may seem easier at times to run, but let me assure you, sticking together and loving each other is much of the essence of our walk as children of God. Virtual reality may be a tremendous tool for the right applications but not for the Kingdom of God. Building strong relationships by continuing to love through difficulties and our differences of opinion needs to be a high priority for all of us. ❖

Chapter 2

Love One Another

In his letter to the Church at Philippi, the apostle Paul is attempting to cause two friends of his, Euodia and Syntyche, to become reconciled. "I plead with Euodia and I plead with Syntyche to agree with each other in the Lord. Yes, and I ask you, loyal yokefellow, help these women who have contended at my side in the cause of the gospel..." (Philippians 4:2-3).

There is no indication in Scripture as to exactly what caused a rift in their relationship. Paul gives no hint as to why these women were not walking in unity. However, we do know enough about Paul to know that this was not a doctrinal issue. If it had been he would have taught them. This was obviously something more trivial. Nevertheless, it was important enough for Paul to address the issue.

Please note that in his request for reconciliation, Paul did not take sides. He pled with each woman to be in agreement. It apparently did not matter to Paul who was ultimately at fault; the matter needed to be cleared up.

There is an important lesson about unity in this brief story: Regardless of who is at fault, being reconciled to one another in love and unity is of utmost priority.

"If it wasn't for people, life in the kingdom of God would be wonderful." I have frequently heard people make this remark in jest. Unfortunately, I fear that many actually believe this statement. We too often choose to ignore people or, at best, simply to tolerate them. This is probably not unlike the relationship that Euodia and Syntyche had. Whatever their reason for disagreement, Paul clearly indicated it was time for them to change their thinking and learn to walk together in love. It is time for *us*, too, to change our thinking and to learn to walk together in love and unity.

The Essence of Unity

Love is the essence of unity. If there is no love there is no unity. As I formulated my initial thoughts concerning this book I realized I could not describe love any better than the apostle Paul.

> If I speak in the tongues of men and of angels, but have not love, I am only a resounding gong or a clanging cymbal. If I have the gift of prophecy and

can fathom all mysteries and all knowledge, and if I have a faith that can move mountains, but have not love, I am nothing. If I give all I possess to the poor and surrender my body to the flames, but have not love, I gain nothing. Love is patient, love is kind. It does not envy, it does not boast, it is not proud. It is not rude, it is not self-seeking, it is not easily angered, it keeps no record of wrongs. Love does not delight in evil but rejoices with the truth. It always protects, always trusts, always hopes, always perseveres. Love never fails. But where there are prophecies, they will cease; where there are tongues, they will be stilled; where there is knowledge, it will pass away. And now these three remain: faith, hope and love. But the greatest of these is love.

(1 Corinthians 13:1-8, 13).

I am convinced that walking in this kind of love would transform the Body of Christ overnight. The problem that we encounter is that we think love is some sort of emotion. We have been taught that love comes and goes depending on moods, age, changes in life, changes in weather, etc. However, none of these are reality.

Love is a Choice

The truth is that love is a choice. Always. We can choose to love or we can choose not to love. Nothing that happens in life can force us to alter whether or not we love someone. It always remains our choice.

When I married my wife nearly 16 years ago I made the choice to love her through the rest of our lives. Nothing that she can do or say can change that decision. The decision is

100% my choice. No outside influences can alter that choice unless I allow them to.

"By this all men will know that you are my disciples, if you love one another" (John 13:35). We all know this passage, but so often we act as though Jesus phrased it differently. Our actions would make it seem as though He said, "By this all men will know that you are my disciples, if you all agree on every point of doctrine." That is not what He said. Jesus clearly told us that people would know we were His followers because we love each other. And love is a choice. It is not whether we all agree on every issue. Even if we disagree on certain points we can still choose to love.

If we within the Body of Christ will make the choice to love the way Paul describes love, we will see a major difference in how the world responds to us and how much we can accomplish within the Kingdom. Let's make the choice to love one another. ❖

Chapter 3

We are One

The book of Joshua contains one of the most profound thoughts in the Bible on how God views His people. It is so radically different from the way we Americans think that it deserves some serious consideration.

The sixth chapter of the book of Joshua tells the story of

the fall of Jericho. The Israelites saw the Lord move mightily on their behalf and the walls of that great city came tumbling down. There was no question that God had done it. Their part was simply to march, blow trumpets and shout; the Lord miraculously handed them the victory.

After that tremendous display of God's strength and power, Joshua and the Israelites found themselves in position to attack the city of Ai. Considering what had just happened at Jericho, Israel thought that conquering this city would be a simple task. It was a much smaller city and not nearly as fortified. This would not really even be a battle for them. They would send in only two or three thousand soldiers. It would be a cakewalk.

Unfortunately, things did not go according to plan. The Israelites were routed. The men of Ai sent the Israelites racing back to their camp. There, seeing they had been overcome, "the hearts of the people melted and became like water" (Joshua 7:5). They knew they had been soundly defeated.

Because of this tragic defeat Joshua is confused. He cries out to God for an explanation. In essence Joshua said, "Lord, I don't understand. What happened?"

God's response gives the full answer to Joshua's question. "Israel has sinned; they have violated My covenant, which I commanded them to keep. They have taken some of the devoted things; they have stolen, they have lied, they have put them in their own possessions" (Joshua 7:11).

If you remember the story, a man named Achan had taken "some of the devoted things." When God was leading them into the promised land He told them there were certain possessions of the people there that they must not keep for personal use. "But keep away from the devoted things, so that you will not bring about your own destruction by taking any of them. Otherwise you will make the camp of Israel liable to destruction and bring trouble on it. All the silver and gold and the articles of bronze and iron are sacred to the Lord and must go into His treasury" (Joshua 6:18-19). Unfortunately, Achan obviously ignored this direct warning.

The real point in this whole incident comes through clearly in the words the Lord uses in addressing Joshua: "Israel has sinned; *they* have violated My covenant which I commanded them to keep. *They* have taken some of the devoted things; *they* have stolen, *they* have lied, *they* have put them in their own possessions." One man, Achan, had done it. Yet God implicates the entire nation.

In our Western culture we often have difficulty fully comprehending biblical concepts because the culture of the people to whom the Bible was written was so radically different than our own. The fact that the Lord would indict the whole nation of Israel for something done by one man does not make much sense to our normal way of thinking. To think this way is completely foreign to us.

However, if you were to go to the Middle East, even today, they would have no trouble understanding this judgement. They do not see themselves as simply a collection of individuals but as families and clans. I have heard the terms "nationhood" or "peoplehood" used to describe this type of mindset — not just a bunch of individuals but all together for a common purpose.

Ultimately, this is how the Lord sees us. Yes, He deals with us on an individual basis, but we are together. He has called us the Body of Christ. We are not to be just a group of individuals all doing our own thing. We are to be working and walking together, to accomplish His purposes. The fact that the Lord would punish an entire nation of people because of the sin of one of those people says a great deal about

His desire for us to be in unity.

We are Infants!

Not long ago I was reading Paul's first letter to the Church at Corinth. Suddenly, words that I had read many times before leapt off the page. "Brothers, I could not address you as spiritual but as worldly — mere infants in Christ. I gave you milk, not solid food, for you were not yet ready for it. Indeed, you are still not ready. You are still worldly. For since there is jealousy and quarreling among you, are you not worldly? Are you not acting like mere men?" (1 Corinthians 3:1-3). What an indictment against the whole American Church! We are seemingly always jealous, quarreling among ourselves. Paul says that when we do this we are infants!

Please understand that in saying this I am also indicting myself. I am just as guilty. However, I am convinced that it is time for us to begin to grow up by making the choice to walk in unity.

And I am not referring to an outward show of affection. We in the Church are often very good at outward displays of "unity."

On my home computer I have a game called "Battle Chess." It is unique in that the chess pieces come to life and actually fight. Of course, the right piece always wins, but each piece interacts differently with each different opponent. Normally a chess game ends when check-mate is reached. This version, however, actually finishes out the game and takes the king at the end. If the queen is the one taking the king, she walks over to him, hugs him and stabs him in the back. That scenario reminds me of some relationships I have seen in the Church! We are often much too ready to put on an outward show of affection while, inside, there is no real unity.

Synergy

The concept I would like to promote through this book is synergy. The dictionary definition of synergy is "the simultaneous action of separate elements which, together, have greater total effect than the sum of their individual effects." The idea is the mathematically impossible equation where the whole is equal to more than the sum of its parts.

Have you ever seen a flock of geese flying in "V" formation? Each goose is aided by the wind break caused by the goose in front of him. When they fly in such a manner geese are able to fly much farther and with much less effort than if they each tried to fly on their own. This is synergy.

I have seen synergy happen on musical recording projects. With today's recording techniques it is possible to take one musician at a time into the recording studio, and, by putting their parts all together at the end, have a full sounding recording. However, if the musicians all work together in the studio there is a recognizable difference in the final production. Again, this is synergy.

I recently read another fascinating illustration of synergy. On the average one farm horse can pull six tons. So if you put two farm horses together how much should they be able to pull? Twelve tons, right? Wrong. Two horses can pull 32 tons! That is synergy. God has put something inherent within His creation that if we will walk together, if we will work together, we can accomplish far more than could each of us doing our own thing.

Even the Bible declares this to be true. "Five of you will chase a hundred, and a hundred of you will chase ten thousand..." (Leviticus 26:8). Mathematically, if five can chase a hundred then a hundred should be able to chase two thousand. But that is not what it says. A hundred can chase *ten thousand*. That is synergy. Again, we must understand that God has made it inherent within His creation that if we will walk together and work together we can accomplish far more than each of us can on our own.

Do you remember the story of the tower of Babel? God's reaction to the people building the tower is remarkable to me. "The Lord said, 'If as one people speaking the same language they have begun to do this, *then nothing they plan to do will be impossible for them'*" (Genesis 11:6). They were all together, working together toward the same goal. Because of this God said that nothing would be impossible for them. How much more should that be true for the Church of Jesus Christ?!

Some time ago I read a statement by George Otis, Jr. about this idea of synergy. "Synergistic unity is to the Church what an unshaven head was to Samson; it is the secret of our strength."[1] Not until we begin to realize the truth of this statement will we, as the Body of Christ, fully accomplish God's plans and purposes for us.

Ultimately, we must realize that God sees us as one, and, therefore, we should pursue unity with all our strength. After all, it is obvious from Paul's statements in 1 Corinthians 3, that our pursuit of unity is a measure of our spirituality. The truth is that, because it is very apparent that synergistic energy is an intrinsic part of unity, it is foolish for us not to pursue unity. If we really want all of the strength God wants us to have in the Church, we simply must endeavor to build unity. ❖

Chapter 4

Pray for Unity

The Old Testament illustrates that God views His people as one. Paul emphasizes again and again the importance of unity to Euodia and Syntyche, to the Ephesians and to us. But one of the clearest pictures of the importance of unity is Jesus on the night He was betrayed.

The book of John records the last prayer Jesus prayed in front of His disciples before His crucifixion. He knew what was coming. The end was close at hand.

Jesus had carefully trained these men for the past three years. Now, it was time for fervent intercession on their behalf. What would He pray? Of all the possible things He could have requested of His Father, what was the highest priority?

"...that they may be one as We are one... that all of them may be one, Father, just as You are in Me and I am in You... I have given them the glory that You gave Me, that they may be one as We are one: I in them and You in Me. May they be brought to complete unity to let the world know that You sent Me..." (John 17:11, 21-23).

Amazing! Jesus did not pray for them to do mighty miracles so that people would be brought into the Kingdom of God. He did not ask the Father to give them supernatural ability to preach the Word. Instead of these He asked that God would protect them and help them to mature; but mostly He simply asked that they would be in unity, that they would be one.

Jesus knew this final prayer would be etched into the disciples' hearts and minds. He knew that He was setting a pattern of how they should pray as they endeavored to walk in the Kingdom of God. Because of this He chose His words very carefully. What He was asking His Father was, "Make them one. Bring them into unity. Open their eyes to the importance of these things. This is what really matters."

In essence, Jesus was asking His Father to fulfill the Word He spoke in Jeremiah: "...I will bring them back... and let them live in safety. They will be My people and I will be their God. *I will give them singleness of heart and action...*" (Jeremiah 32:37-39).

For Us Today, Too

Jesus goes on in His prayer to clearly state, "My prayer is not for them alone. I pray also for those who will believe in Me through their message" (John 17:20). He was praying the same thing for us! This was not just for the disciples that Jesus handpicked while He was physically here on earth. His prayer was also for His disciples today who have believed through their message. This means you and me. We, too, are to understand that unity, and praying for unity, is not a side issue. It is a top priority. Jesus' prayer not only reveals how deeply He desires unity for us, but it also serves as an example to us of the importance of praying for unity.

Jesus set the pattern; it is time for us to learn to follow it. Praying for unity must become a major emphasis for us. This should be true both in our personal lives as well as in corporate times of prayer. Just as Jesus made it a major theme of His prayer in John 17, we should also consistently pray for unity.

The Church in America today spends far more time talking about prayer than doing it. We absolutely must become more resolute in prayer. Specifically, we must begin to pray fervently for unity.

Perhaps a good place to begin in praying for unity would be with the words of the popular song, "One Voice," by Robert Gay:

Father, we ask of You this day come and heal our land.
Knit our hearts together that Your glory may be seen
*   in us.*
Then the world will know that Jesus Christ is Lord.

Let us be one voice that glorifies Your Name.
Let us be one voice declaring that You reign.
Let us be one voice in love and harmony;
And we pray, O God, grant us unity.

I once talked to a Lutheran pastor who told me an interesting story about how prayer can effect unity. For several years he and his church had been crying out to God for revival. During prayer one day he felt the Lord spoke to his heart, "I cannot give you what you are asking for, because if I do, you will use it against the other churches in town."

"What do You mean, Lord?" asked the pastor.

"You already tell everyone that your church is *the* church. If I were to give you an outpouring of My Spirit you would use that as ammunition to prove your stance."

"God, I didn't realize. What should we do?" he asked.

"Pray for the Methodist church down the road."

The pastor confided to me that this was probably the most difficult thing God had ever asked of him. At that point in his life he would have rather been martyred than to pray for revival to come to a Methodist church. However, he was obedient and began to pray for the church. Within a few months the Methodist church had a new pastor and revival broke out. Within two years their attendance had tripled.

Through all of this the Lord taught the Lutheran pastor a very serious lesson about unity and prayer. God is not so much interested in blessing our little projects. He wants to bless the Church. Not a particular denomination. Not a particular congregation of people. The Body of Christ.

It is time for us as the people of God to stop simply praying for our own little sphere of influence. We still need to continue those prayers but we must broaden our scope. We should pray for the new believers in Eastern Europe. We should pray for the leadership of the Church in Africa. We should pray for the church down the road that believes a bit differently than we do on certain issues. We need to pray for unity and have unity in our prayers. Hidden here is a key that will help unlock the door that keeps unity out of the Church.

"The effectual fervent prayer of a righteous man availeth much" (James 5:16b). Our prayers have power.

We should ask the Lord to do again what He did in 2 Chronicles 30:12. "...the hand of God was on the people to give them unity of mind to carry out what the king and his officials had ordered, following the word of the Lord." If the Lord did it once He can surely do it again. Pray that this type of "unity of mind" would come upon the Church of Jesus Christ today.

We must make it a point to pray for true unity to come to the Body of Christ. If we really want unity, then we must follow Jesus' example and pray for it fervently. ❖

Chapter 5

Admit That We Need One Another

Another vital step in truly walking in unity is to admit our need for our brothers and sisters in the Lord.

> Now the body is not made up of one part but of many. If the foot should say, "Because I am not a hand, I do not belong to the body," it would not for that reason cease to be part of the body. And if

the ear should say, "Because I am not an eye, I do
not belong to the body," it would not for that
reason cease to be part of the body.

If the whole body were an eye, where would
the sense of hearing be? If the whole body were an
ear, where would the sense of smell be? But in fact
God has arranged the parts in the body, every one
of them, just as He wanted them to be. If they were
all one part, where would the body be? As it is,
there are many parts, but one body. The eye cannot say to the hand, "I don't need you!" And the
head cannot say to the feet, "I don't need you!"

(1 Corinthians 12:14-21)

We need one another!

Unfortunately, this entire concept of needing one another is contrary to what our American society has taught us.
In our culture independence is a virtue. We immortalize our
founding fathers who fought and paid dearly for their independence from England. John Wayne, Mr. Independent, is
our idea of the great American hero. We are taught from an
early age to stand on our own two feet. "Get going. You can
do it!" we are told.

However, the longer I walk with the Lord the more I am
convinced that our Creator did not design us to make it on
our own. The above verses from 1 Corinthians not only
suggest but insist that we need each other. The minute you
begin to believe that you are strong enough to make it all by
yourself you have set yourself up for a fall. We are the Body
of Christ. There is no hand anywhere on earth that has
enough strength to survive if it is severed from the rest of its
body. There is no member of the Body of Christ that is strong
enough for the long haul without the rest of the Body. We

need each other.

A few months ago I was ministering at a church and the music team shared a song that was written by their pastor. The song is entitled "We are His Body":

We are His body, to Him we belong.
I am a part of you, together we are strong.
Through you He speaks to me. Through you He heals.
Through you He comforts me. Through you I know He
     is real.
So take time to pray. Take time to say, "I love you."
Take time to let me know that you'll be thinking of me.
'Cause I need to know that you'll always stand beside me,
And that you'll always let the Master work through you.

© 1992 Marshall Townsley.

In every situation we need to remember that we are the Body of Christ. This is not always easy. However, Paul's first letter to the Church at Corinth tells us a bit about true Christian love. "Love... always protects, always trusts, always hopes, always perseveres. Love *never fails*..." (1 Corinthians 13:7-8).

Let's Be Honest

Have you ever heard the Twila Paris song, "The Warrior is a Child"?

They don't know that I go running home when I fall down.
They don't know who picks me up when no one is around.
I drop my sword and cry for just a while
'Cause deep inside this armor, the warrior is a child.

© 1984 Singspiration Music/ASCAP.

Can I be really honest for a moment? Sometimes I feel like that. Please understand that the Lord has allowed me to grow very strong in Him. I have to be as I am on the road ministering two or three weekends every month. But sometimes I just need people to love me. It is so wonderful to have people minister to me after I have seemingly given all I have to give. We need one another.

We even have a Scriptural injunction to watch out for and take care of one another: "See to it, brothers, that none of you has a sinful, unbelieving heart that turns away from the living God. But encourage one another *daily* (author's emphasis) ...so that none of you may be hardened by sin's deceitfulness" (Hebrews 3:12-13).

We must understand that we all have a part to play in the Body of Christ. Sometimes we are giving, sometimes receiving. We cannot, however, simply distance ourselves from the rest of the Body and expect to survive. We need each other.

Some time ago I visited the school (kindergarten through grade 12) that is affiliated with our church. As I walked in there was a young lady, probably in tenth grade or so, sitting there who was obviously in emotional turmoil. I asked her if she was okay and she began to cry. As her tears flowed I talked with her for a few minutes then I said, "You know what? Right now you need someone to be strong for you and pray for you. I'd like to do that. Maybe two months or two years down the road I'll need you to be strong for me and pray for me, but right now you need me to be strong for you. Can I pray for you?" She agreed and I did. That is a part of what the Body of Christ is all about. We need each other.

Those Who are Different

One of the most difficult tasks that God has given us is to walk in unity with those who are different than us. Paul addresses this issue in 1 Corinthians 3:4-7. This section follows immediately after the verses we looked at earlier where Paul calls them infants because of their jealousy and quarreling. "For when one says, 'I follow Paul,' and another, 'I follow Apollos,' are you not mere men? What, after all, is Apollos? And what is Paul? Only servants, through whom you came to believe — as the Lord has assigned to each his task. I planted the seed, Apollos watered it, but God made it grow. So neither he who plants nor he who waters is anything, but only God, who makes things grow."

The Lord had instilled in Paul certain gifts and abilities, specific strengths that made him unique. God also put unique gifts and abilities within Apollos. The people then took those characteristics, the specific attributes that the Lord had built within these men, and used them as reasons for division. They had totally missed the point. We have differences in order to complement one another, not to divide. If we were all exactly the same we would not get very far in accomplishing God's plans and purposes.

So often we want everyone else to be exactly like us. What a tragedy that would be. I have had the opportunity to know some extremely gifted men and women over the years. Some were marvelously gifted in music. Some were amazing visionaries. Some were extraordinary teachers or counselors. Some had excellent administrative or organizational gifts. Many were even multi-talented, having tremendous gifts in several areas. However, I have yet to meet one person who has it all. And I know I never will because we all have need of one another.

Church to Church

This whole concept of needing one another is just as true on a church-to-church basis as it is on an individual basis.

Local churches must begin to put aside their doctrinal differences in order to win the lost to Jesus. Is it more important for us to agree on the proper method of taking the Lord's Supper or to preach the gospel? We too often act just like the Church at Corinth.

A couple years ago I encountered a study entitled *A.D. 2000*. This report profiled 788 different plans to evangelize the world by the year 2000. To me just that fact is amazing — 788 *different* plans! But what was most amazing was the results of the study:

- nearly 2/3 were either non-cooperating or only partially cooperating with other groups to fulfill their work.
- only 10.5% considered cooperation with like-minded traditions and bodies indispensable.

Nine out of ten thought there was some chance they might evangelize the entire world by the year 2000 all by themselves!!! What a haughty attitude! We cannot make it on our own. We were not designed to make it on our own. We need each other.

> The truth of the matter is that God's universe has operated on the principle of interdependence from the very beginning. Atomic structure, the human body and the family unit all testify to this truth. From one end of creation to the other, nothing is strong enough to operate with total autonomy. The Trinity is, in fact, the first and best network. Its members are at once equal in value and standing, but diverse in their roles or expressions.[2]

In order to truly walk in unity it is absolutely essential for us to admit our need for one another. We cannot walk about in an attitude of independence when the Scriptures are clear that we are to be interdependent. We need each other. ❖

Chapter 6

Be Willing to Follow Leadership

One of the main keys for walking in unity is to be willing to follow leadership.* After I wrote most of this chapter I went back and carefully reread it. I realized that this is potentially the most controversial section of this book. Our American society has inundated us with the idea that we are to question authority. Most of us have been taught from a very early age that we are to be independent. The idea of following leadership to the fullest measure is foreign in our society.

Therefore, the easy thing to do with this chapter would be to reject many of the ideas because they are not what we are accustomed to. I would suggest, rather, that we judge the Scriptures and principles shared from the perspective of what is true and right, not from what we have been taught by a post-Christian America.

Too often today the Scriptural ideal for following leadership does not coincide with our way of doing things. Because we are so tainted by our oft-repeated cultural slogan, "question authority," we are usually amazed that even when King Saul pursued David and threatened his life, David still absolutely refused to harm the king because the Lord had placed Saul in that position. Today we might look at Saul and say that he should be killed. At the very least we would suggest that he should be removed from office, forcibly if necessary. David knew better.

In the twenty-third chapter of Matthew, Jesus launches into a tirade against "the teachers of the law and the Pharisees." Throughout the rest of the chapter Jesus calls them such names as "hypocrites," "blind guides," "snakes" and "vipers." Obviously Jesus did not think very highly of these men. However, at the beginning of the chapter He makes a statement to the people that is mind-boggling. "'The teachers of the law and the Pharisees sit in Moses' seat. *So you must obey them and do everything they tell you...*'" (Matthew 23:2-3). He then begins to tell these leaders what horrendous people they really are. But He prefaces His diatribe by telling the common people that they must obey the Pharisees and teachers of the law. Even though they are not perfect, they are still to be obeyed. Even though they are terribly misguided (not the same as rebellious), they are still to be followed. This is not quite the way we think today.

A Lesson From Narnia

A while back I was reading C.S. Lewis' *The Chronicles of Narnia* to my son. In the second book, good Prince Caspian, the rightful heir to the Narnian throne, and his band of renegade talking animals are about to engage in battle with the evil king. Caspian has in his possession a magical horn that will summon help in the time of greatest need. Because he perceives that they have reached that time, he is ready to blow the horn. Unfortunately, he has no idea what form the help will take or to where in the land of Narnia the help will be summoned. After careful discussion the leaders agree that the "help," whatever it may be, will arrive in one of three places. Because they are presently situated at one of those places, Caspian needs two messengers to go stand watch at the other two locations. He asks for volunteers, and two dwarfs speak up. One, Nikabrik, adamantly and gruffly refuses any thought of going. At this, Trumpkin, the other dwarf, who has repeatedly stated that he did not believe the horn would actually cause any help to come, speaks up.

"Thimbles and thunderstorms!" cried Trumpkin in a rage. "Is that how you speak to the King? Send me, Sire, I'll go."

"But I thought you didn't believe in the Horn, Trumpkin," said Caspian.

"No more I do, your Majesty. But what's that got to do with it? I might as well die on a wild goose chase as die here. You are my King. I know the difference between giving advice and taking orders. You've had my advice, and now it's time for the orders."[3]

Author Larry Christenson further illustrates this point in his book, *Back to Square One*. Christenson tells of a football team that turned their huddles into a discussion time. Everyone offered his own idea of what play should be called and how it should be run. When the coach found out he sternly rebuked them. The quarterback was to be the only one talking in the huddle. If the others had ideas they could share those on the way to the huddle, but once in the huddle there was to be one voice — that of the quarterback. The coach had trained him how to call plays and the coach had confidence in his abilities. The coach went on to explain that listening to one voice was the only way the team would move ahead in a united manner.

Sometimes Christian people have to put up with a "second-best" plan. God allows that to happen. The perfect plan doesn't always take place in an assembly of God's people because those in positions of authority might not always see things as clearly as they ought to. That is one of the reasons leaders should always be open to counsel. Other "team members" may have important input which will help them arrive at a better decision. But any coach will tell you that it is better to use a second-best play and execute it well than to fumble through one that might have better potential.

This issue is so important with God that He allows people to come into a position where He says, "Accept this second-best plan, one that you don't personally agree with. It's more important for this team to get together than for your particular play to be used, even if it is a good one." With this approach we can move against the enemy with unity and strength.[4]

Obey Your Leaders

Scripture does not just allude to this idea but spells it out plainly: "Obey your leaders and submit to their authority..." (Hebrews 13:17).

Recently I received a newsletter from well-known teacher Bob Heil. He addressed this issue of being willing to follow leadership.

In the hotel room in Krakow, Poland, Gary Dinnell spoke very seriously to our little group of twelve. Gary had been on several trips into the Soviet Union to help pastors in the underground Church. Now he was giving us guidelines about how we should act when we were with those leaders. He said the pastors we were going to meet had all been in prison. Many had been tortured for the faith. "These men," Gary said, "are highly respected by the people in their congregations and by the Church in general."

Then Gary made his main point, "If Bob Heil, who is our leader, says it's time to go, don't say, 'Let's just stay a few minutes more,' or 'Surely we can make it if we stay another half hour here.' Don't question, don't do anything that challenges Bob's authority in front of the brethren. That would shock and disgust them, especially the leaders of the underground Church. Discussions about choices or decisions only happen when the leader invites them to happen."

Being thus warned, we travelled on into the Ukraine and then to Moscow. By the time we reached Moscow we all realized that the American custom of everyone speaking forth his own ideas on any subject was very prevalent in our group. As a result, my position as leader was indeed damaged in the sight of a few of the leaders in the Soviet Union.

I, myself, found it very hard to be a leader. I hadn't been the kind of leader who simply makes decisions and leads the way in many years. Our little group would repeatedly end up in long discussions over even trivial things: whether we should take this route or that; should we go by plane or train; who will arrange for the tickets; who should see about getting a new tire for the trailer, etc. Rather than being the leader of the group, I became the coordinator of the discussions. Everyone seemed to have good, valid reasons for changing or altering any decisions I might make.

On our second day in Moscow, as I was reading Paul's first letter to Timothy, I was struck by the authority with which Paul spoke: "This charge I command you..." (1 Timothy 1:18); "I do not allow..." (2:12); "Have nothing to do with..." (4:7); "I solemnly charge you in the presence of God..." (5:21).

I suddenly realized that we in the United States have been robbed of a great deal of corporate or united strength. We seldom defeat the demonic "strong man" standing over our communities (Luke 11:21-22; Daniel 10:13). We are severely limited in our corporate impact and witness. While "two can put ten thousand to flight," we must be united in order to do that. Part of being united is being in submission, both to one another and to the leader over you.[5]

We too often simply do not understand the biblical view of submitting to leadership.

Even in the Midst of Imperfection

Let me explain that the local church I am a part of is not a perfect church. We cannot be. We are human beings. I frequently offer my advice before a decision is made. However, I am fully committed to the people and the leadership. Once the decision is made, once the play is called, I am going with it. It is the only way we will move ahead in a united manner.

Am I comfortable with everything that happens at our church? Of course not. There are mistakes, even major mistakes. There are decisions made that I am certain I could improve upon. But I am committed to the leadership and I understand, just like Trumpkin the dwarf, that "I know the difference between giving advice and taking orders. You've had my advice, and now it's time for the orders."

It is often amazing to me to watch the chain of events that happens when a local church is seeking new leadership. The scenario often goes something like this:

1. The congregation prays fervently for God to send them His appointed leadership.
2. God answers their prayers and sends the person(s) He wants in charge.
3. Somewhere along the way the new leadership, because they are human, makes one too many mistakes and the congregation becomes disgruntled.
4. The people begin to murmur.
5. The leadership leaves, willingly or unwillingly.

6. The entire process starts over.

The bottom line is this: Do we believe that the Lord heard and answered our original prayer or not? If so, we absolutely must accept the leadership He has given, even with their flaws.

Please understand that in all of these illustrations I am not talking about leaders who are in direct rebellion to the Word of God. If you perceive a problem you should be willing to go and talk with the leader in question. Jesus gives very clear instructions in Matthew 18:15-17 of how to handle a situation where we believe we have been wronged.**

I am referring to those who are endeavoring to do their best to follow the Lord. However, even those with whom we disagree, even those who may be misguided in certain areas, are still to be submitted to. Remember Jesus' command to the people regarding the Pharisees: "you must obey them and do everything they tell you" (Matthew 23:3). Remember Hebrews 13:17: "Obey your leaders and submit to their authority. They keep watch over you as men who must give an account. Obey them so that their work will be a joy, not a burden, for that would be of no advantage to you."

I am absolutely convinced that the Church will never reach unity as God intends until we learn the lesson: Commitment to church leadership is not just a good idea, it is a direct command from The Coach. ❖

---

* Please understand that this chapter does not address the entire concept of proper leadership. Leadership is much too weighty of a topic to do justice to in this small volume. However, let me

offer a couple of thoughts for leaders. First, although as leaders we scripturally have the authority to lead our people and command their obedience (Hebrews 13:17; Matthew 23:2-3), we must not lord it over them (Matthew 20:25-28; Mark 10:42-45; Luke 22:25-27). Ask for their input. Request their assistance in making major decisions. Second, be humble in your position (2 Corinthians 1:24). People are far more willing to follow servant leaders than heavy-handed dictators. See "Questioning Correctly" chapter for further thoughts.

** It is also possible for leaders to offer too much input into the personal lives of their followers. In this case, again, Matthew 18:15-17 is appropriate. See "Questioning Correctly" chapter for further thoughts.

Chapter 7

Give Up Our Opinions for the Sake of Unity

Opinions. Everyone, especially in our society, has lots of them. "Everyone is entitled to his own opinion," is a popular catch-phrase. We consider our opinions sacred.

Some time ago I visited a church where the pastor was preaching on unity. His text was Ephesians 4:1-6. When he shared verse two: "Be completely humble and gentle; be patient, bearing with one another in love," he said that the Greek phraseology has the connotation of giving up our own opinions. He said that sometimes true unity involves setting aside our opinions. When he made this statement he stopped and looked out at the congregation. Then he raised his voice and demanded, "My what?! My opinion?! That most holy of all things, my opinion?!"

Of course he was being facetious, but we all got the point. We often think that our opinions are the most important things in the whole world. If anyone dares to suggest that our opinions might be misguided we are quick to take issue. We are willing to be challenged on the color of our car or how well we can play baseball or bake cookies, but never try to challenge us on our opinions!

A major part of the Kingdom of God here on earth is how we interact with our brothers and sisters in Christ. "Do nothing out of selfish ambition or vain conceit, but in humility consider others better than yourselves" (Philippians 2:3).

Let's be honest for a moment. Are there certain passages in the Bible you would prefer to ignore? The passage above is sometimes like that for me. "...*consider others better than yourselves*", "But God, she's wrong and I'm right!"

The truth of the matter is that the Church today spends large quantities of time arguing over whose interpretation of certain Scripture passages is the most accurate while the enemy of our souls leads the people of the world down the pathway to eternal torment.

In light of this it is amazing to me that we within the Church can persist in attitudes which declare that we individually have all the right answers. When will we realize that, at best, we are but a small part of the Body of Christ? Declaring that, "I know what is best for this church" or "I have the answer for how things should be done" is simply a matter of arrogance. We too frequently believe that our theological ideas are the most sound, our attitudes the most proper, our hearing of God's voice the most accurate, our understanding of His Word the most correct. We think that if everyone would simply line their thinking up with ours that all of the world's (or at least the Church's) problems would be solved. Honestly, this is haughty, arrogant pride to the maximum degree!

What is Most Important?

During the last several years you have undoubtedly changed your opinions on many things. We all have. Our ideas of acceptable fashions, proper management, the best way to raise vegetables, the best way to raise children, how the church should be run, even our interpretations of Scripture have all, at one time or another, changed somewhat. Of course, we now have all of these things (and practically everything else in life) figured out. However, do you suppose that there is any chance that in the next several years, just as in the previous several years, you will change any of your closely held opinions? Opinions on any subject, even how we interpret certain Scripture passages? Any chance at all? Of course there is. However, if several years from now we look back and we have left behind a bloody battlefield fighting for our strongly held opinions what have we gained? But if we look back and can say that we chose to walk in love, is that not much more pleasing to God?

Let me explain that I have often struggled with this concept. Being a very black-and-white person, I have lots of opinions. If you have a topic, I have an opinion. However, I am more and more convinced that standing up for my closely held opinion on a topic has far less value than choosing to lay those opinions aside for the sake of unity.

Some time ago I read an article written by a youth pastor. He stated that parents of teenagers often came to him to discuss a problem they were having with their son or daughter. When this happened he consistently counseled the parents to "major on the majors and minor on the minors." What he was saying was that if the "problem" was a clear violation of Scripture or something that could potentially harm the child or others, then he suggested they address the issue forcefully. If it was only a secondary issue, something of little or no long-term consequence, then he told them not to be so strong.

One day the youth pastor's son came home wearing an earring. Dad almost went through the roof. He did not like his son wearing an earring. He dreaded what the people at his church would think. It had to go.

Then he remembered his oft-given advice, "major on the majors and minor on the minors." He realized his son wearing an earring was, really, only a side issue. All things considered his son was a good kid. Why risk causing him to rebel by making a major case out of something so minor?

We could all learn something from that father. Too often I have encountered people who become disgruntled in church because the service lasted longer than usual. My pastor addressed this awhile back at our church. "If the Communists are lining your family up to be shot, that's a major concern. If the service lasts ten minutes longer than normal, that's not."

Everyone Has an Opinion

I recently heard of a church split that occurred because of a disagreement over the color of carpet in the sanctuary. We spend too much time majoring on the minor points. What eternal difference does the color of the carpet make? Is it worth dividing a church over?

Music is one of those areas that everyone has an opinion about. Unfortunately, each person is absolutely certain that his opinion is right. Recently a friend of mine, Fern Batchelor, sent me something she had written for her church. Fern leads worship at a church near Philadelphia, Pennsylvania.

The Perfect Worship Service

After listening carefully over the past several years, we believe we have finally determined what those who attend our church really want in music. Following are the items that come up most frequently whenever this topic is discussed:

- more fast songs in the opening praise time and more slow songs in the opening praise time.
- more of those wonderful, lovely old hymns and less of those stupid, dead old hymns.
- a longer and shorter time of praise at the beginning of the service, and a shorter and longer time at the end.
- songs to flow quickly into each other and long periods of time between songs for reflection.
- more repetitions of songs so they can be learned and meditated upon while singing, and less repetitions of songs because it gets boring singing the same thing over and over.
- more of those lovely arrangements with extra instruments and less of those showy arrangements with all those instruments.
- to sing the good old songs more often and to stop always singing those same old songs.
- songs to be sung in higher and lower keys.
- the band to play in the middle of the platform

> where they can be seen, back behind the plants
> where they won't be a distraction, louder, softer,
> faster, slower, more often and not at all.

Are you beginning to understand that ultimately every one of us have numerous opinions that we believe are valid? We all have lots of opinions on lots of topics. However, for the sake of real unity it is time to lay aside our opinions and simply love one another.

Help Instead of Challenge

Recently I came across a tremendous quote by Harry Ironside that capsulizes this entire concept:

> It is very evident that Christians will never see eye
> to eye on all points. We are so largely influenced
> by habits, by environment, by education, by the
> measure of intellectual and spiritual apprehension
> to which we have attained, that it is an impossibil-
> ity to find any number of people who look at
> everything from the same standpoint. How then
> can such be of one mind? The apostle himself
> explains it elsewhere when he says, "I think also
> that I have the mind of Christ." The "mind of
> Christ" is the lowly mind. And, if we are all of *this*
> mind, we shall walk together in love, considering
> one another, and seeking rather to be helpers of
> one another's faith, than challenging each other's
> convictions.[6]

We may as well admit that Mr. Ironside is right — we will never all agree on everything. My wife and I have been married for almost 16 years. We married young, so at this point we have been married nearly half our lives. We have experienced many things together. But even with all of this going for us we occasionally disagree with one another's opinions. Does this diminish our love for one another? Absolutely not. We realize that choosing to love each other is more important than always agreeing with one another. Sometimes it is even necessary for my wife and me to put aside our opinions for the sake of walking together in unity.

This is true for the Church also. We absolutely must realize that it is essential for us to stop quibbling over our opinions and, instead, choose to walk together in unity. ❖

Chapter 8

Questioning Correctly

"I urge you, brothers, to watch out for *those who cause divisions and put obstacles in your way that are contrary to the teaching you have learned.* Keep away from them. For such people are not serving our Lord Christ, but their own appetites. By smooth talk and flattery they deceive the minds of naive people" (Romans 16:17-18).

One thing I do not wish to promote through this book

is some sort of zombie-like, passive, I-am-programmed-to-do-exactly-as-I-am-told type of people. Sometimes we must confront error. Martin Luther would never have nailed his 95 theses to the door of the Wittenburg church if he had adopted a totally non-confrontational attitude. However, knowing exactly when and how to address error has always been one of the most difficult issues within the Church. Let me attempt to offer a few thoughts on this subject.

First, we must understand the difference between truth and perception. I recently heard Ben Kinchlow, co-host of the 700 Club television program, speaking at a church. He made the comment that perception is stronger than truth. By way of illustration he said that if we meet someone and our perception is that the person is evil, whether or not he truly is evil is of little consequence. To us he is evil. Our perception may be totally opposite from the truth; but in a confrontation in our minds, our perception always wins out.

The evidence of this can be seen again and again in everyday life. Our perception of situations, people, and ideas will always sway our reaction to those things. Just as in Ben Kinchlow's illustration, we may find out later that our perception was totally in error, but at the time it becomes reality to us.

We need to understand this because it can be very easy for us to decide to confront someone we believe is in error. However, all too frequently we find that our perception was wrong. Unfortunately, at this point it is too late — the damage has been done. When we choose to confront error we must be absolutely certain that we are not simply acting from just our own perception of the situation.

Maintaining Humility

One of the things we must always maintain is a humble, teachable attitude. I know a man who is a highly respected teacher in the Body of Christ. He is a very scholarly man. He understands both Greek and Hebrew and has spent many years studying the Scriptures. Over the years I have seen him powerfully teach truth from God's Word. I have also heard him give his opinions on certain topics, even on Bible passages, but always he emphasizes that these are opinions. He is careful to separate things that are very plain in the Word of God and things that are not. I refer to this as doctrinal humility.

Most of us today are sorely lacking in this area. We are certain that the things we believe are correct, and we often spend large amounts of time lobbying others to agree with our perspective. We gather a following and feel that the larger the following the more correct we must be.

David's son, Absalom, thought like this. Through well-thought-out plans he carefully garnered the support of the people of Israel. Through four years of lobbying to gain their allegiance the Bible says that Absalom "...stole the hearts of the men of Israel" (2 Samuel 15:6). He was then ready to proclaim himself as king. The plan worked so well that David ran for his life.

Unfortunately, this is the same way that most church splits and other major divisions in the Church come about. Sometimes openly, sometimes behind the scenes, troops are rallied to support a cause. We may not always plan as carefully as Absalom. Perhaps a passing comment is made. Or a statement is shared out of "concern." But all the while the end goal of "I am going to win" is in the heart.

There are two main causes of division in churches. Sometimes churches split over issues of power (like Absalom's case). Sometimes splits are caused by doctrinal disagreements. Even when the surface issues seem petty, the underlying issue is ordinarily either one of power or doctrine.   And the idea of rallying forces is usually the main downfall. Instead of honestly and openly discussing issues, we lobby for our positions behind the scenes.

Understanding True Heresy

The important thing to remember in all of this is that the heart attitude is critical. Someone who proclaims false doctrine is not necessarily a heretic. That person is, of course, in error, but they are only being heretical (in the true New Testament Greek understanding of the concept) if they are endeavoring to gather followers. Let me explain.

The word "heresy" comes from a Greek word that we transliterate as "hairesis." It means "a choosing, choice; then, that which is chosen, and hence, an opinion, especially a self-willed opinion, which is substituted for submission to the power of truth, and leads to division and the formation of sects; such erroneous opinions are frequently the outcome of personal preference or the prospect of advantage."[7] The definition of "heretical," the adjective form of heresy, offers further insight: "...causing division by a party spirit, factious."

We are not wrong to offer our thoughts on Scripture interpretation. In fact, leaders should, just as the man I mentioned previously, maintain doctrinal humility. We should all preserve that attitude within ourselves. The problem comes in when we campaign for our ideas rather than discuss issues. We are too ready to make alliances rather than talking through difficult questions. We frequently marshal support to our side instead of prayerfully seeking the Lord and maintaining a humble, teachable attitude.

A further definition of the Greek word for heresy is this: "a predilection either for a particular truth, or for a perversion of one, *generally with the expectation of personal advantage.*"[8] Personal advantage. There is the bottom line: We have not yet fully died to self, so we want self to be correct. To do this we gather a following.

In Acts 20, Paul is leaving Ephesus for the last time and is addressing the elders there. "I know that after I leave, savage wolves will come in among you and will not spare the flock. *Even from your own number men will arise and distort the truth in order to draw away disciples after them.* So be on your guard!" (Acts 20:29-31). Note here that they are not just distorting the truth. They are doing it to "draw away disciples after them." This is very much in line with the above definitions of heresy.

Paul addressed this issue from a different perspective in his first letter to the Corinthians. Some of the people had opted to cause divisions by choosing to follow either Paul or Apollos. In essence Paul said, "Don't do it!" "I planted the seed, Apollos watered it, but God made it grow. So neither he who plants nor he who waters is anything, but only God, who makes things grow" (1 Corinthians 3:6-7). If you read this entire section in context Paul is saying, "Stop looking at men, look at God. Don't divide yourselves, be united in Christ."

Galatians 5:19-21 lists out "acts of the sinful nature." The list consists of things like "sexual immorality," "idolatry," "witchcraft," "hatred," etc. Along with these are also listed some things we do not usually think of in the same context as these. There are things like "discord," "dissensions," and "factions." These things are just as heinous to the Lord as the others.

Please understand again that it is not wrong to question things you do not understand or do not agree with. However, we must always maintain a proper attitude in our questioning.

In the midst of writing this I have been embroiled in a very serious debate over a divisive issue. Something was being taught that had great potential for division. After looking into the issue a bit I found that the person doing the teaching had not researched any other viewpoints. I confronted him with this information and a very heated discussion followed. We quickly realized that neither of us was making any headway and parted company. However, I called him later and told him that although I maintained my questions about the teaching, my attitude had definitely been wrong. I apologized and asked him to forgive me. He readily accepted my apology and extended forgiveness.

Our attitude in these things is what makes all the difference. This is especially true if we are questioning someone who is in a leadership position. If God has put that person in position we must be very careful how we treat them. Our actions should reflect the words of the apostle, Paul, as he wrote to the church at Philippi: "Let your gentleness be evident to all" (Philippians 4:5).

Perhaps Paul's words to Timothy would be appropriate to close this section. "Preach the Word; be prepared in season and out of season; correct, rebuke and encourage — *with great patience and careful instruction*" (2 Timothy 4:2). Always maintain that great patience and careful instruction. ❖

Chapter 9

Build Friendship Relationships

Friends. What does that word bring to your mind? Hope-fully you find it a pleasant word, one that offers real comfort. That is truly what friendship is all about.

Do you remember the story of Jonathan and David? Theirs is a story of real friendship.

Jonathan's father, King Saul, tried to kill David. Jonathan knew nothing about this, and, when David insisted it happened, tried to convince David that there must have been some mistake. Nevertheless, even in the midst of a disagreement, Jonathan said, "Whatever you want me to do, I'll do for you" (1 Samuel 20:4).

Later, during the same conversation Jonathan pledges his allegiance to David for the rest of his life (1 Samuel 20:13-15). The Scripture even says that Jonathan loved David "as he loved himself" (1 Samuel 20:17).

Because David had married Saul's daughter, Michal, he was always on hand for special feasts at the king's table. At the next family gathering Saul noticed that the place David usually sat was empty. Saul asked Jonathan why David was absent. Jonathan explained that David had asked for permission to go visit his family and Jonathan had granted his request.

> Saul's anger flared up at Jonathan and he said to him, "You son of a perverse and rebellious woman! Don't I know that you have sided with the son of Jesse to your own shame and to the shame of the mother who bore you? As long as the son of Jesse lives on this earth, neither you nor your kingdom will be established. Now send and bring him to me, for he must die!"
>
> "Why should he be put to death? What has he done?" Jonathan asked his father. But Saul hurled his spear at him to kill him. Then Jonathan knew that his father intended to kill David. Jonathan got up from the table in fierce anger; ...he did not eat, because he was grieved at his father's shameful treatment of David.
>
> (1 Samuel 20:30-34)

Saul was saying, "Listen, kid, if you don't help me get rid of David you won't ever have a kingdom for yourself." However, it is obvious that David's friendship was of far more value than was a kingdom to Jonathan.

Just a few verses later David and Jonathan part company for the last time. Before they do, however, they once more pledge their undying friendship.

> Jonathan said to David, "Go in peace, for we have sworn friendship with each other in the name of the Lord, saying, 'The Lord is witness between you and me, and between your descendants and my descendants forever.'" Then David left, and Jonathan went back to the town.
>
> (1 Samuel 20:42)

Later, when Jonathan dies in battle, David mourns his friend. "I grieve for you, Jonathan my brother; you were very dear to me. Your love for me was wonderful, more wonderful than that of women" (2 Samuel 1:26).

Our Society's Idea of Friends

This picture of true friendship is all too rare today. Our society tells us that people are to be used as stepping stones to higher levels of power and prestige. Too often the value in friendships is how much money can be gained from them.

Jesus refutes this modern ideology in John 15:13. "Greater love has no one than this, that he lay down his life for his friends." *"Lay down my life? But what do I get out of it?!"*

The Bible teaches us that friends are valuable simply for their friendship.

When we have true, biblical friendship relationships we automatically bypass many of the things that can hinder our being in unity. If we really love one another and care about one another as people, we are less concerned with the short-comings of others, both real and perceived.

About a year ago, after ministering at a church, I went to lunch with the pastor. During the course of the conversation he mentioned that they had previously had a bit of friction between two members of their church's staff. The reason stemmed from the fact that one was very outspoken and often shared his feelings freely. The other person was much more reserved and did not necessarily want to hear the feelings of the other, especially as those feelings related to her ministry abilities.

After explaining the situation the pastor told me that the problem had been solved. "Do you know how we did it?" he asked.

"No, but I'd like to," I responded.

He explained that one day the entire staff spent the day together at an amusement park. The two who were occasionally at odds with one another spent a great deal of time together during that day. They got to know each other. They became friends. The problem was solved because friends care for one another.

Becoming Friends

I have long espoused this concept and have made it a vital part of the music ministry at our church. I am keenly aware that creative, artistic-type people are very given to competition. Unfortunately, this is even true in the Church. Because of this, one of my main goals is to get the people involved in our music ministry to like each other, to care about each other. If I can do this, the competitive mentality diminishes. Friends are not interested in serious competition with one another. Friends want to see each other succeed.

Frequently, various members of the music ministry of our church get together for a meal or just to visit. We spend time together, even occasionally during our rehearsal time, just getting to know one another. The relationships being built during these times automatically carry over into ministry times.

Our church's music ministry has an annual tradition. After prayer, worship and sharing with just the members of the music ministry, everyone goes home and gets their families. We reconvene about 30 minutes later and *party*. We eat, play volleyball, talk, play party ping-pong under black lights and just generally enjoy one another. There are no spiritual connotations to the whole thing, and yet there are all the spiritual connotations possible because we are growing in our friendships with each other. And those friendship relationships will impact our ministry times together. We are more united because we care about each other.

This type of relationship building is not just for those involved in music ministry. It should be a vital ingredient in the lives of all of us. Spending time with others, talking, sharing and listening, should be a normal part of life for us as believers.

A while back I heard a pastor read a poem. Unfortunately he did not know the source of the poem (someone had read it to him), but I quickly wrote it down as he read it:

Oh the comfort of feeling safe with a person,
Having neither to weigh thought nor measure word
But letting it all out, chaff and grain together;
Knowing that a faithful friend will sift it
And keep what is worth keeping,
And, with a breath of mercy, blow the rest away.
© unknown

We all need friends like that. No masks. No pretending. People we can be real with.

This poem reminds me of some of the words of Solomon. "Wounds from a friend can be trusted..." (Proverbs 27:6) True friends are not out to get us. Often close friends speak truth that wounds our fragile pride, but since we rest assured that they have our best in mind, we can accept what they have said.

"...the pleasantness of one's friend springs from his earnest counsel" (Proverbs 27:9). A friend will not hold back the truth — he is earnest, and that is good.

The closer we in the Church can be as friends the more unity we will have. Surface relationships are part of life, but we should always be trying to deepen those relationships. My pastor regularly makes a statement that we are trying to live out at our church: "It is less important for us to be known as a friendly church than it is for us to be a church that makes friends." We need to be friends with one another.

The apostle Paul had many friends. His friends took care of him while he was in prison (Acts 24:23; 27:3). He regularly referred to various close friends in his letters, extending greetings from them or asking that greetings be extended to them. He even refers to some as his "dear friends" like Timothy, Luke and Gaius. If Paul, the great man of faith that he was, found it necessary to have close friends, should not we also consider this a high priority?

Degrees of Friendship

Please understand that I am not talking about having close, intimate relationships with everyone you know. There are various levels of relationships. Even Jesus demonstrated this. There were multitudes that followed Him, but He had twelve that were closest to Him. Of these there were three,

Peter, James and John, that comprised Jesus' inner circle. Even beyond this the Bible refers to John as "the disciple that Jesus loved" (John 13:23; 19:26; 20:2; 21:7; 21:20). Jesus did not have the same closeness with everyone that He did with John.

The same is true for us. We will not have the same depth in all of our relationships. Sometimes we will have a relationship like Ruth and Naomi in the Bible. "...where you go I will go, and where you stay I will stay. Your people will be my people and your God my God. Where you die I will die, and there I will be buried. May the Lord deal with me, be it ever so severely, if anything but death separates you and me" (Ruth 1:16-17). Other times our relationships may not be quite so strong.

However, we should be striving to deepen all of our relationships. We will never be extremely close to everyone we know, but if we endeavor to become at least a little closer with each one then we will be much closer to walking in unity. ❖

Chapter 10

Walk in Forgiveness Toward One Another

Suppose you owe a debt of one million dollars. If the debt is not paid within one week you face the certain penalty of a lifetime in prison. You have absolutely no resources with which to pay the debt. No rich uncles. No lottery tickets. No Publisher's Clearinghouse Sweepstakes. Nothing.

During the entire week you cannot sleep. You try to sleep, but instead you lie awake trying to think of any possible way of coming up with the million dollars. If you sell your house, your car, all of your furniture, your stamp collection, your dog, and your time-sharing agreement on the house at the lake, you still come up $887,423 short. It looks hopeless.

For the whole week you have difficulty eating because your stomach is churning with worry. You are irritable and cranky. You feel boxed in. There seems to be no hope.

Ultimately, the day of reckoning arrives. As you are being driven to the courthouse you are still trying to come up with some grand scheme to pay back the money. When you arrive at your destination you again realize the hopelessness of the situation. It's over. The rest of your days will be lived out in prison.

You sit silently in the courtroom, wondering whether it might be worth making a break for the door in an attempt to escape. But then, before you have the chance, your name is called.

You stand and the full weight of the situation hits you like a freight train. You nearly crawl to the front, crying uncontrollably.

The judge asks if you have the money to pay.

"No sir," you sob.

In a detached, unemotional voice the judge announces, "Lifetime in prison. No chance for parole. Next case."

In the next half-second of silence your mind races, considering what the sentence means and how it will impact those you love. Suddenly, out of a combination of terror and brokenness you cry out, pleading with the judge for mercy.

There is total silence in the courtroom. The judge stares at you then once again looks over the papers that represent your case. He motions for the court clerk to come forward.

They confer in hushed tones. Then the judge looks back at you.

"Not guilty. You're free to go." He smiles.

Before the judge has the opportunity to change his mind you practically run out the door. You feel as though a giant weight has been lifted from your shoulders. You are simultaneously laughing and crying.

As you half dance and half float out the door you bump into an old friend. Excitedly you proceed to share with him what has just happened you. Suddenly you remember that about eight years ago you lent this friend five dollars and he has never repaid it. Your joy turns to anger as you demand payment. He assures you that he will pay you but he simply does not have any cash with him right now. You will accept no excuses. You want it *now*. You call over a nearby police officer and insist that he arrest the man.

The Unforgiving Servant

Of course I am simply retelling the parable of the unforgiving servant from Matthew 18:23-35. Jesus told the story of a servant who had just been forgiven a great debt when he encountered a fellow servant who owed him a minor debt. Instead of offering forgiveness as he had received, the servant had him thrown into prison.

When we look at this story we find it difficult to relate to. We cannot conceive of ourselves doing anything so harsh, even if we were in a similar situation. The finale is absurd. How could anyone who had been on the receiving end of such compassion possibly act in such a cruel manner?

Yet nearly every Christian acts out this same scenario on a regular basis. We have received the most amazing pardon ever. Not only were we completely guilty but we continue to be guilty. We daily commit treason against the

King. We do not deserve mercy, but God — because of Jesus' suffering and death — freely gives it. However, after we have received the most unthinkable absolution imaginable we turn around and refuse to forgive others. Ridiculous!

Jesus actually shared his unforgiving servant parable after Peter asked Him how many times he should forgive someone. "Then Peter came to Jesus and asked, 'Lord, how many times shall I forgive my brother when he sins against me? Up to seven times?' Jesus answered, 'I tell you, not seven times, but seventy-seven times'" (Matthew 18:21-22). Jesus then went on to illustrate this point by way of the story.

The apostle Paul made a comparable statement in Ephesians. "Be kind and compassionate to one another, forgiving each other, just as in Christ God forgave you" (Ephesians 4:32). "*...just as in Christ God forgave you*"!

How much forgiveness does the Lord extend to you? How much should we extend to one another? "But he's gone too far this time, Lord." What if God had that attitude with us?

How Much Forgiveness Does God Give Us?

One of my favorite song lyricists is Ed Kerr, formerly with the music group "Harvest." On his solo debut album, "Unexpected Turns," there is a song entitled "I Never Doubt."

Warnings ignored, cautions unheeded.
I've seen the signs and yet I walk on.
I call You my Lord, I cry out how I need You,
But deep in my heart commitment seems so small.

And I wonder if I dare to breathe that prayer again.
Surely this time my rebellion's gone too far.
But I never doubt the sun will greet me in the morning.

I never wonder if the rain will wash the earth.
Just as certain as the sun I see
It is certain that You care for me
And Your love will wash away my sin again.

These words depict God's heart toward us. Even when we are faithless, He remains faithful (2 Timothy 2:13). How much forgiveness, then, should we offer each other?

"Bear with each other and forgive whatever grievances you may have against one another. Forgive as the Lord forgave you" (Colossians 3:13).

Choosing to Not Be Offended

One of the best ways I have found to walk in forgiveness is simply to choose to not be offended by people's words or actions. This, honestly, makes walking in forgiveness easy. If we never allow the words or actions of others to cause us to be upset or bitter, then forgiveness is simple. Let me illustrate.

A friend of mine leads worship at a large church. Several years ago a few members of the staff of the church, my friend included, were conducting a series of services in another city. During one of the evening meetings the pastor had given an altar call. The pastor was out near the front of the platform praying for people, the piano player was playing softly in the background, and my friend, the worship leader, stood waiting for the next time he would lead the congregation in song.

At one point the pastor turned to the worship leader and asked him to sing a song that the piano player was playing. Somewhat sheepishly, my friend admitted that he did not know the song. At this statement the pastor pointed his finger at the worship leader and very forcefully said, "Learn it." With that he turned back around and continued praying for people.

Stop for a moment and put yourself in the position of the worship leader. What would you have done? It would be very easy to be offended in such a situation.

My friend chose to not be offended by his pastor's comment. He thought, "Maybe the last person pastor prayed with gave him a difficult time. Whatever the reason, I make the choice to not be offended by his remark." At that moment he forgave the pastor. Then he simply put it out of his mind.

The next day the pastor and worship leader passed each other in the hall of the hotel where they were staying. The pastor stopped my friend and said, "Brother, I'm sorry. I had no right to speak to you that way yesterday. Will you forgive me?" Of course he extended forgiveness. However, he found it very easy to do so because he had harbored no bitterness. He had already forgiven when the incident occurred. Even if the pastor had never apologized, my friend had already forgiven him and had made the choice not to be offended and harbor bitterness.

I find so many people today who talk about how they were offended by this person's comment or that person's actions. We can only be offended if we allow ourselves to be. Is being offended really anything more than feeling justified for being angry and bitter toward someone? Next time you find yourself in a situation that could be offensive simply do what my friend did; make the choice to not be offended. Forgive before bitterness takes root. Whether or not the other person ever apologizes then becomes a moot point. You will harbor no bitterness because you chose to forgive immediately.

Jesus clearly told us how God expects us to forgive in the prayer that we commonly refer to as "The Lord's Prayer."

He taught His disciples to pray, "...Forgive us our sins, for we also forgive everyone who sins against us..." (Luke 11:4). The Greek sentence structure here is clearly saying that we are asking to be forgiven of our sins *because* we forgive those who sin against us.

Honestly, what would happen if the Lord forgave us in the same way we forgive others? Consistently walking in forgiveness toward one another is a vital key for unity. ❖

Chapter 11

Honor One Another

Often I have heard of automobiles, works of art or other artifacts being sold at an auction for astronomical prices. A single signature on a letter from a deceased dignitary can bring tens of thousands of dollars. A car previously owned by a well-known celebrity can sell for as much as a million dollars or more.

This same concept can be seen in the homes of average people all over the world. We all possess certain items that have a great deal of sentimental value to us. Because of this we would find it hard to part with these items regardless of how much money is offered.

I once heard an interesting conversation along these lines. A man was saying that he did not know what he would do if his home was ever lost to fire or flood. To this comment another queried, "You have insurance, don't you?"

"Of course," the man replied, "but no amount of money could replace some of the items that have been given to me over the years."

The interesting thing is that in all of the above scenarios someone who did not have the same sentimental attachment could look at any of these items and find them of little or no value. The raw materials that make up the item are of relatively little worth. So what makes the items themselves so valuable? Just this: what someone is willing to pay for them. The items, in and of themselves, are worth very little. But because someone is willing to pay such a high price for them, the items automatically have value.

The same is true for you and me. We have little or no intrinsic value. In reality, because of our sinful nature, we have almost no inherent worth. However, God was willing to give up His only Son, Jesus, to pay for us. Suddenly, we have become valuable, not because of anything inherent within us, but because God was willing to pay such a tremendous price for us. No intrinsic value. No inherent value. But an enormous value because of what God was willing to pay.

In my living room at home we have a table that was given to us. If we were told that the table was purchased at WalMart for twenty dollars, how would we probably treat the table? Like an ordinary piece of furniture, right?

However, if the person giving us the table told us it was a very rare antique that was purchased at an estate sale for twenty-thousand dollars, would we treat that same table any differently? Of course we would. We would most assuredly be very careful with it. We would probably make mention of its great worth to visitors in our home. It would hold a higher place of honor in our minds.

I would suggest that in the same way we must learn to honor, respect and esteem one another in the Kingdom of God, not because we have anything of worth in the natural but because the Lord has valued us so highly. As the Lord values us, so we should value one another.

The Old Violin

Have you heard the Wayne Watson song, "Touch of the Master's Hand"? It is a song about a violin being sold at an auction. The violin looks beaten and worn so the auctioneer offers it for just a few dollars. A few people bid on it half-heartedly.

While the bidding is still going on an elderly gentleman makes his way to the front, picks up the violin and tunes it. Then he begins to play beautiful melodic strains on the instrument. The auctioneer stops and listens. Surprisingly, he dramatically raises the bidding from a few dollars to a few thousand dollars. The people are shocked. They ask the auctioneer why it is suddenly worth so much more. He states simply, "It was the touch of the master's hand."

We must realize that the Lord of all creation paid the most phenomenal price imaginable for each one of us. He placed such a high value on us that He gave up His only Son to purchase us. How then should we value one another?

We must realize that how we value one another is always our choice. I can choose to abuse the table in my living room, even if it is worth $20,000 (by the way, it is not worth that much). The choice of how I want to value and esteem that table is completely up to me.

The same is true in the Church. God will not force us to honor one another. We have the option of not having respect or esteem for each other. No one will coerce us to cherish our brothers and sisters in the Lord. However, it is the right thing to do.

"Do nothing out of selfish ambition or vain conceit, but in humility *consider others better than yourselves*" (Philippians 2:3).

A Prophet Without Honor at Home

This idea of honoring one another is foreign to us. We are very willing to esteem and regard people for great heroic or athletic feats or for outstanding intellectual achievement. But to simply honor others in everyday life, especially those to whom we are closest, is not something that is normal for us.

Even Jesus found this to be true. One day He was in His hometown and found the people had no honor or respect for Him there.

> Coming to His hometown, He began teaching the people in their synagogue, and they were amazed. "Where did this man get this wisdom and these miraculous powers?" they asked. "Isn't this the carpenter's son? Isn't His mother's name Mary, and aren't His brothers James, Joseph, Simon and Judas? Aren't all His sisters with us? Where then did this man get all these things?" And they took offense at Him. But Jesus said to them, "Only in his hometown and in his own house is a prophet without honor."   (Matthew 13:54-57)

He was just Jesus, the carpenter's son. They remembered

Him from when He was a boy. He was not special, just a kid from the neighborhood. They did not respect or esteem Him.

I find this to be true also. It is amazing to me how much worth we in the Church put on someone who comes from far away. I teach regional worship seminars at churches all across the nation. We average just under 100 people at our seminars. However, the smallest seminar I have ever done was hosted by a church just ten miles from my home church. There I was not the "prophet from a far country." I was just Tom. Just like in Jesus' case above, there was no honor.

I am convinced that we must begin to learn to honor one another more, even those with whom we are very familiar. "Be devoted to one another in brotherly love. Honor one another above yourselves" (Romans 12:10).

Honor Through Trials

Many years ago some friends of mine were going through some major struggles in their lives. Some of the things that had happened had caused them deep heartache and grief. Because of this, some other friends and I decided to honor them. We gave an extremely elaborate dinner and they were the very special guests. It would take far too much time and space to give the details here but let me just say that we honored them in a big way. Their circumstances did not change overnight. However, because they knew we esteemed them highly and were standing with them they were able to face the situations more easily.

Since that time we have had the opportunity to esteem many others with banquets, parties, surprises and more. These are all great ideas but honoring one another does not need to be an elaborate production. It can be very simple to show others that we place a high value on them. A simple note or a card for no special occasion can show great respect and honor for another person. A positive word of affirmation can display much esteem for someone.

The important point in all of this is not so much the outward demonstration of honor. The outward manifestation will be a natural by-product of consistently endeavoring to raise the value of others in our own minds. We must realize anew the tremendous price Jesus paid for those around us. That will automatically give them far more value in our own eyes.

Honoring one another is a giant step toward walking in unity. ❖

Chapter 12

Believe the Best About One Another

Several years ago I was eating dinner at the home of a friend of mine, a respected leader within the Body of Christ. During a momentary lapse in the conversation his teenage daughter told him of the recent moral failure of a local pastor with whom my friend was acquainted. Being a guest in the home I was a bit uncomfortable with this dinner conversation. My initial thought was, "How will he react to the news about this man?" My friend's response was far different from anything I expected. He simply looked up, smiled and said that he would not believe it unless the man told him himself. With that he continued eating.

I sat there silently wondering what would happen next. My friend's daughter was dumbfounded. She objected strenuously. She knew the daughter of the man. This was not hearsay. It was rock-solid information. Besides all this, how could her own father doubt her word?

My friend calmly sat his fork down, looked her straight in the eye and explained, "Honey, it's not that I don't believe you. It's just that I have chosen to believe the best about my brothers and sisters in the Lord in every situation. Unless he tells me himself I won't believe it."

I could have heard a thousand sermons or read hundreds of books on this subject and not have been as deeply affected as I was by seeing it lived out before my eyes. My friend had chosen to believe and speak the best in love and nothing — absolutely nothing — would persuade him otherwise.

The message was clear: Believing the best about our brothers and sisters in the Lord is of utmost priority.

Communist Tactics

Before the iron curtain fell in Eastern Europe, one of the tactics of the Communists to destroy churches was to separate the people and tell them lies about each other. Often the believers refused even to listen to the lies, but occasionally some succumbed. They began to believe the lies and soon distrusted their own Christian brethren. What a tragedy that the people had not been taught this simple foundational principle: Always believe the best about one another.

Jesus said that the people of the world would know that we were His disciples by our love for one another (John 13:35). True Christian love... "always protects, always trusts, always hopes, always perseveres. Love *never fails*..." (I Corinthians 13:7-8). As a part of our love for each other, then, we should always believe the best about our fellow Christians regardless of the circumstances.

In this country today we have no Communist leaders speaking lies to us, yet I see a similar willingness to believe lies and breed disunity in the American Church. For example, events of organizations like Operation Rescue are usually horrendously distorted by our national media. Reports of the same events by the Christian media seem so contrary to the secular media it is as though they are not even reporting the same event. Yet some Christians choose to believe the secular media's coverage and find fault with their brothers and sisters. What a shame.

I have seen the same thing on a local and national scale within the body of Christ. We are far too ready to accept anything we hear as truth, especially that which is negative, regarding our brothers and sisters in Christ. This is even more of a reality for those in "lime-light" ministries. It is almost as though we want to see them fall. How tragic.

It even happens regularly in our churches. "Psst. Hey, did you hear what so-and-so did?" And we listen and believe it, regardless of how damaging or harmful. Simply accepting information as truth is damaging enough to the party being discussed. However, when we believe wrongly about a brother or sister, we are also harming ourselves. "The words of a gossip are like choice morsels; they go down to a man's inmost parts" (Proverbs 26:22). If we listen and believe we can destroy our own spirit!

Those Who are Different

Most of us have within ourselves the capacity to believe the best about those we like. However, we all know at least one person, even within the Body of Christ, whose personality and mannerisms are either so different or so similar to our own that we have trouble agreeing with them even when we agree with them. These are the people we usually have the most trouble believing the best about. However, I am more and more convinced that we should make a conscious effort to believe the best about *all our brothers and sisters* in every situation.

One thing that has helped me immensely in this area is simply understanding that people are different. Different people have different personalities. Because of this we can have real trouble understanding the thinking and/or actions of someone whose personality is radically different from our own.

A number of years ago I worked with two men who had very different personalities. One was a by-the-book organizational type. Each task needed to be done in a certain way. Any variation from this and it was wrong. The other man was a tremendous visionary. He was extremely spontaneous. Organization was a foreign concept to this guy. He was much more at home in the midst of chaos.

When the three of us were together in organizational meetings I often ended up mediating because the two of them rarely understood each other. They were both speaking English but they often needed an interpreter since their ways of thinking were so radically different.

Please understand that in saying these things I am not finding fault with either one. Both were extremely gifted men. My point is that until we realize that many people on earth are vastly different from us in personality *and that there is nothing inherently wrong in that* we will often be frustrated by others. (If you do not yet understand that the Lord purposely made us different go back and reread the "Admit that We Need One Another" chapter of this book.)

Endeavoring to Understand One Another

Some time ago the elders of our church each took part in a well-respected personality test. Honestly, I found nothing terribly surprising in the results, but it did help us all understand one another a bit better. We are now more fully aware of why each one thinks the way he does and how that affects his input on major decisions.

I would suggest that if you are not at least somewhat aware of various personality types you might consider some further reading. *The Spirit-Controlled Temperament* by Tim LaHaye (Tyndale House Publishers) gives clear concise definitions of the four basic personality types. Additionally, *The Two Sides of Love* by John Trent and Gary Smalley (Focus on the Family Publishing) covers the same concepts in a different fashion. Both of these resources can be very helpful.

In endeavoring to believe the best about one another our attitude should be that of Paul in his letter to the church at Philippi. "Do nothing out of selfish ambition or vain conceit, but in humility consider others better than yourselves" (Philippians 2:3). The KJV says: "...let each esteem the other better than themselves." Not just those who are easy to esteem but even those who are not.

We must each convince ourselves that believing the best of our brothers and sisters in Christ is absolutely essential. We must remove phrases like "It was bound to happen" or "I always thought there was something not quite right about that person" from our thinking. It is essential for us to uphold, love and support one another both for our own sake as well as for the sake of the Body of Christ. ❖

Chapter 13

Encourage
One Another

Often as we read the Bible, we overlook what we would
refer to as "the little things." We want to know more
about the weightier matters and miss the day-to-day topics.
One of these that we so often neglect is the manner in which
we talk to one another.

One day Jesus told His followers, "You have heard that it was said to the people long ago, 'Do not murder, and anyone who murders will be subject to judgement.' But I tell you that anyone who is angry with his brother will be subject to judgement. Again, anyone who says to his brother, 'Raca,' is answerable to the Sanhedrin. But anyone who says, 'You fool!' will be in danger of the fire of hell" (Matthew 5:21-22).

The word "raca" (rā'cǎ) literally means "empty head." Today, our equivalent of this word would be "airhead." Jesus is telling the people that simply calling one another names puts them in danger of judgement!

The normal form of verbal interaction in our society is put-downs: cutting remarks designed to destroy one another, or, at least, to bring others down a notch or two. The truth is that we in the Church should be doing the opposite. We have enough detractors in the world. From one another we need encouragement.

It is amazing to me how frequently the Bible refers to this idea. Throughout the book of Acts, the apostle Paul is consistently encouraging the churches. Not long after being stoned and left for dead he was once again encouraging the believers (Acts 14:22). Immediately after he and Silas were sovereignly released from the Philippian jail they went to Lydia's house where the Christians were meeting and "encouraged them" (Acts 16:40). Numerous other times Paul encouraged his brethren.

Paul even frequently sent others to churches in various cities for the express purpose of encouraging those people (Ephesians 6:21-22; Colossians 4:7-8; 1 Thessalonians 3:2).

"Son of Encouragement"

One of Paul's early travelling companions and fellow ministers of the gospel was named Joseph. You probably remember him by the name the apostles called him: Barnabas. Why did the apostles use this name? The Scriptures do not give a specific reason. However, Acts 4:36 tells us that the name Barnabas means "son of encouragement." It is safe to surmise that Barnabas was such an encouraging person that they gave him a nickname. We should all be sons of encouragement.

The Bible even refers to God as an encourager. Acts 9:31 tells us that the Church was "strengthened and encouraged by the Holy Spirit." In Paul's second letter to the Thessalonians he told them that God "by His grace gave us eternal encouragement" and then goes on to pray that the Lord will continue that encouragement (2 Thessalonians 2:16-17). There are other passages that refer to the Lord as our encourager, but I think you get the picture. We in the Church need to rid ourselves of the all-too-frequent cutting remarks and, instead, become encouragers.

Several years ago I was teaching an all-day worship seminar. At one point I finished a section of teaching and asked for questions. I was amazed when several of those asking questions offered lightly-veiled criticism aimed at those with whom they ministered. Unfortunately, it became obvious that the people being talked about were present.

As I listened and responded I could not help feeling deep sorrow for the people making the comments as well as those at whom they were directed. There was no encouragement, only tearing down. Paul tells Titus to: "Remind the people... to slander no one, to be peaceable and considerate, and to show true humility toward all men" (Titus 3:1-2).

Without question, one of the things sorely lacking in our society today is encouragement. Encouragement among close friends is a rare commodity. Between those who are not so close it is usually non-existent.

The Power of Encouragement

Yet despite all of this, I am constantly amazed at the power of an encouraging word. A simple, "You can do it," spoken to my eight-year-old son, David, can be transforming. A brief encouraging phone call to someone who is having trouble can make a world of difference. Sharing with the people around you what you appreciate about them will have a powerful long-term effect.

One of the best things you can do to encourage people is to look for their strengths. One night at our home fellowship group the leader took half of the people into another room and gave them an "assignment." Those of us who remained behind had no idea what those who were taken had been asked to do. When they returned, each person who had been given the assignment began to share with another person. They shared why they appreciated us as friends. They shared about the strengths they saw in us. They shared about specific times when we had been of help to them. It was a *very* encouraging time.

The idea, we found out later, was simply to encourage. It was powerful.

Later, as we discussed what took place with the entire group, it was interesting to note that very few of us really felt comfortable. Both the encouragers and those receiving encouragement were a bit uneasy. However, we all agreed that the benefit of encouragement is worth the effort.

Sometimes we have difficulty encouraging others because we are not quite certain what to say. We may be afraid we will sound silly. However, we do not need to wait for big events or accomplishments to give a word of encouragement. We can even comment on the little things our friends say or do that we appreciate. In so doing, we will undoubtedly bless them as well.

In his book, *You Gotta Keep Dancin'*, Tim Hansel shares a letter from a former student. Allow me to quote a brief portion of that letter.

> I may not be burned deeply into your memory, Tim, but you are in mine. And now that you've surfaced once again in my life, I thought I'd let you know that.
>
> I remember the first day I had you for P.E. when I was a freshman in 1966. We all had to run the 600-yard dash and I didn't want to. I was always coming in last, no matter how hard I ran (and I always ran as hard as I could). But this one was different.
>
> Oh, I still came in last — by about 150 yards, as I remember. But I remember you running along side of me that last 100 yards yelling, "Good effort, Lou! Great effort! Absolutely magnificent..."
>
> I felt like I'd won the Olympic Gold Medal for the marathon. And I became totally devoted to you because no one had ever encouraged me like you.[9]

Encouragement is far more powerful than most of us understand.

At our church we utilize a worship band playing music that is a bit more contemporary in nature than most traditional churches. One of our main keyboardists is a former organist from a very traditional denominational background. When she first started playing keyboard for us her style of playing was considerably different from the style of music we were playing. However, I realized very quickly that she was not only a true worshipper but was very skilled and creative with her music. Every time she did anything that was even a bit more contemporary than her traditional background I commended her for it and encouraged her to continue on. Partly because of my encouragement, she has used instructional videos and attended teaching workshops on keyboards. She is now as comfortable playing a contemporary style of music with no sheet music as she is playing out of the hymnal. She is even teaching others. Encouragement can make a world of difference.

The Bible even gives us direct commands to encourage one another. "Therefore encourage one another and build each other up..." (1 Thessalonians 5:11). "But encourage one another daily..." (Hebrews 3:13). "...let us encourage one another..." (Hebrews 10:25).

If we will consistently endeavor to encourage one another it will go a long way toward promoting unity in the Church. ❖

Chapter 14

Speak Well of One Another

E qually important as the way we speak *to* one another is how we speak *about* one another. Proverbs 6:16 says that there are seven things that the Lord hates. Verse 19 lists the last of these as "a man who stirs up dissension among brothers."

To really comprehend the full impact of this statement we must understand something about the character of God.

He never does anything half-heartedly. His love is so all-encompassing that He gave up His only Son for the sake of the people He created. The Bible often refers to "the zeal of the Lord." He does nothing with only partial feeling. Everything He does is full of passion. If this is true, then what must God's hatred be like? And yet it says the Lord hates "a man who stirs up dissension among brothers."

Unfortunately, in my travels, I regularly hear music team members speak extremely negatively about their worship leader. I have heard ministers of music speak negatively about their pastor. Even husbands or wives often make negative comments about their spouse.

In her book titled *A Mother's Touch*, Elise Arndt describes what she did when she caught her children speaking harshly or negatively toward one another.

> The way we have learned to handle this particular
> problem in our home is by counteracting every
> bad word with a good one. We base this on
> Philippians 4:8: "Finally, brethren, whatever is
> true, whatever is honorable, whatever is right,
> whatever is pure, whatever is lovely, whatever is
> of good repute, if there is any excellence, and if
> anything worthy of praise, let your mind dwell on
> these things." When a derogatory word is said
> about another person I make the person who said
> it counteract it by saying something especially
> nice about that one.[10]

What would happen if we made this a practice in the church?! Every time someone in the Church makes a negative comment about another person we should immediately ask them to say something nice about that person. I would be willing to wager that we could wipe out negative comments within one month.

Do Not Judge One Another

The Bible is very clear about how we are to talk about one another. "Brothers, do not slander one another. Anyone who speaks against his brother or judges him speaks against the law and judges it. When you judge the law, you are not keeping it, but sitting in judgement on it" (James 4:11). If we are busy judging others we are missing God's plan for *our lives*.

I recently read an interesting fictional book entitled *The Portal*. In it two friends, Nathan and Denise, are taken from our world to a land called Fayrah in another dimension. Besides the physical differences in this land, the major difference in Fayrah from our world is that no one criticizes anyone else. Everyone speaks words of encouragement to each other.

Once there, they become separated and Nathan begins to say bad things about Denise. Each time he does a horrendous pain shoots through Denise's head and body.

One of the inhabitants of Fayrah, Aristophenix, tells Denise that the pain must be because Nathan is saying bad things about her. He explains in his poetic talking style:
"Your words can cut
and force others to bleed,
'cause they're spoken from mouths
which have been Image-Breathed."

As the reality of what Aristophenix was saying hit her, Denise responded, "You mean Nathan is doing all this to me with his mouth? This is all happening because of what he is saying?"

Her companions nodded.

"Great authority have Upside Downers (earthlings). Powerful very, their words of blessing or cursing."[11]

The Power of Our Words

These thoughts echo the words of Solomon. "The mouth of the righteous is a fountain of life..." (Proverbs 10:11). We should choose our words carefully in order to bring life, not pain and death.

"Reckless words pierce like a sword, but the tongue of the wise brings healing" (Proverbs 12:18). Our words can actually help bring healing and restoration.

"The tongue that brings healing is a tree of life, but a deceitful tongue crushes the spirit" (Proverbs 15:4). Let us decide together to not crush anyone's spirit with our words.

"The tongue has the power of life and death..." (Proverbs 18:21). *Life and death!*

I recently encountered the pastor of a nearby church at the post office. I have ministered at his church on several occasions and he and I know one another very well. He mentioned that the week prior he had been talking with some believers from another church. During the course of the conversation one of them began to share some very destructive rumors he had heard about my pastor. My friend immediately stopped the man and told him that the rumors were not true and that he would do well to check out rumors before spreading them any further. This should be essential advice for the Church. "He who covers over an offense promotes love, but whoever repeats the matter separates close friends" (Proverbs 17:9).

Psalm 15 is one of the shortest psalms in the Bible. It contains only six verses. Verse one asks the question, "Lord, who may dwell in Your sanctuary? Who may live on Your holy hill?" In our modern vernacular we might phrase it, "Who can come before God?"

The rest of the psalm gives character traits of those the

Lord deems acceptable to come before Him. Verse three says, one who "has no slander on his tongue, who does his neighbor no wrong and casts no slur on his fellow man." God does not want us slandering or casting a slur on our brothers and sisters in the Lord.

The Right Way to Handle It

Scripture is also very clear on the proper way to handle the situation if we believe someone has sinned against us:

> If your brother sins against you, go and show him his fault, just between the two of you. If he listens to you, you have won your brother over. But if he will not listen, take one or two others along, so that "every matter may be established by the testimony of two or three witnesses." If he refuses to listen to them, tell it to the church; and if he refuses to listen even to the church, treat him as you would a pagan or a tax collector.
>
> (Matthew 18:15-17)

Spreading rumors is never acceptable. In the verses above Jesus very plainly spells out the appropriate action to take when we believe we have been wronged. Do not tell everyone else about it first. Go to the person and confront him. If that does not work then take two or three others with you the next time. However, you must still be talking *to* the person, not spreading rumors about him. Anyone unwilling to take these simple steps has absolutely no business spreading stories, true or untrue, about another person.

We must be very careful with our words. "With the tongue we praise our Lord and Father, and with it we curse men, who have been made in God's likeness. Out of the same mouth come praising and cursing. My brothers, this should not be" (James 3:9-10).

Speaking well of each other is an absolute necessity for building unity in the Body of Christ. ❖

Chapter 15

Be Patient
With One Another

Be completely humble and gentle; be patient, bearing with one *another in love"* (Ephesians 4:2).

Recently I read an article about a woman named May Lemke. When she was 52-years-old, having raised five children of her own, she agreed to take in a six-month-old infant named Leslie. Mentally retarded and without eyes, Leslie also had cerebral palsy. He was totally unresponsive to sound or touch. His parents had abandoned him.

May spent the next 18 years loving Leslie, endeavoring to teach him the simple tasks of life. Nothing was second nature to Leslie. The things we take for granted, like eating and walking, took him many years to develop. During this time May consistently prayed over Leslie, asking God to show her how to help him develop.

One day she noticed Leslie "pluck" a taut string around a package. Based on this action she began to fill the house with music. She consistently had music playing during their waking hours. May and her husband, Joe, even bought an old upright piano. She repeatedly pushed Leslie's fingers against the keys to show him that he could make sounds with his fingers. During all of this Leslie remained totally indifferent.

Then it happened. One morning at 3 a.m. May was awakened by the sound of Tchaikovsky's Piano Concerto No. 1. She shook Joe and asked if he had left the radio on.

"No," he said.

May went immediately to Leslie's room. She found him sitting at the piano, smiling. He had never gotten out of bed on his own before. He had never seated himself at the piano. He had never voluntarily or deliberately struck the keys with his fingers. Now he was playing a concerto — and with deftness and confidence.

From that point Leslie's musical abilities developed. He went on to play piano at churches, civic clubs and schools, colleges, county fairs and, finally, network television.

Because of May's love and patience, an abandoned child that our society would label as "worthless," was able to offer hope and happiness to thousands of people.[12]

In light of this story I would like to pose a question: When did Jesus come and save us? The answer, of course, is when we were dead in our sins. "But because of His great love for us, God, who is rich in mercy, made us alive with Christ even when we were dead in transgressions..." (Ephesians 2:4-5). He took us from a sentence of death, just like May did for Leslie, and gave us life. He placed such a high value on us that He gave His very life that we might live.

If God views us in such a manner then how should we view one another? How should we treat one another?

We Have Nothing That Was Not Given to Us

Not one of us has anything of any value that did not come from the Lord (1 Corinthians 4:7). Yet we so often find it easy to look down on others we perceive as different from ourselves. For some reason we often think we are better than someone else.

Perhaps you know someone you perceive is only at the stage where they are plucking the string on the package. What is your reaction to that person? Are you willing to be patient with him? Will you allow him to continue growing and maturing without belittling him? If someone saw you as being at that particular stage in your walk with the Lord, how would you want them to treat you?

"Here is a trustworthy saying that deserves full acceptance: Christ Jesus came into the world to save sinners — of whom I am the worst. But for that very reason I was shown mercy so that in me, the worst of sinners, Christ Jesus might display His unlimited patience as an example for those who would believe on Him and receive eternal life" (1 Timothy 1:15-16). Jesus displayed *unlimited* patience *as an example* for us! He showed us how to do it so that we might have patience with others.

Just for a moment think about some of the things that God has been working on in your life for a long time. If you are like me you can probably list several. Perhaps you struggle with:

- evil thoughts
- lack of compassion
- rudeness
- lack of patience
- lust
- bad temper
- greed
- lack of trust in God or others
- continual tardiness
- desire for power or prestige
- or any of numerous other possibilities

How long has He been working on one or more of these areas in you? Maybe God has been working on some of these areas in you for a very long time.

Now think about a trait or characteristic that really irks you in an acquaintance of yours. Perhaps you might recall someone with a short temper. Or someone who is chronically late. Or someone who constantly reminds others of their shortcomings. Will you be as patient with that person as God has been with you? Or will you insist that the person make a drastic and immediate change?

We too often expect immediate changes in others even though the Lord offers us *unlimited* patience.

Patience and Pearls

Sometimes God uses those irksome qualities in other people to strengthen us. We must learn to have patience or we will blow up. In his book, *Growing Strong in the Seasons of Life*, Chuck Swindoll talks about trials and patience. In this context he refers to how oysters form pearls. An irritant — a grain of sand — slips inside.

On the entry of that foreign irritant, all the resources within the tiny, sensitive oyster rush to the
spot and begin to release healing fluids that otherwise would have remained dormant. By and by
the irritant is covered and the wound is healed —
by a *pearl.* No other gem has so fascinating a
history. It is the symbol of stress — a healed
wound... a precious, tiny jewel conceived through
irritation, born of adversity, nursed by adjust-
ments. Had there been no wounding, no irritating
interruption, there would have been no pearl.
Some oysters are never wounded... and those who
seek for gems toss them aside, fit only for the stew.

No wonder our heavenly home has as its
entrance *pearly* gates! Those who go through them
need no explanation. They are the ones who have
been wounded, bruised, and have responded to
the sting of irritation with the pearl of adjustment.

J.B. Phillips must have realized this as he
paraphrased James 1:2-4:

> *When all kinds of trials crowd into your
> lives, my brothers, don't resent them as in-
> truders, but welcome them as friends! Real-
> ize that they have come to test your
> endurance. But let the process go on until
> that endurance is fully developed, and you
> will find you have become men (and women)
> of mature character...*[13]

Having this type of response to the shortcomings of
others — not resenting them — will help us become more
patient over the long haul. In the process we will find pearls
of mature character forming within us.

Long-Suffering

Although I much prefer to use a more modern translation of the Bible, occasionally the old English words of the King James Version are more descriptive than the current vernacular. The most common Greek word that the modern translations render as "patience" is used 13 times. Two of those times the KJV uses the word "patience." The other 11 times the translators chose the word "long-suffering." Although we no longer use this word in modern society, to me it is a very graphic word: "to suffer long." It gives a bit more insight into patience that we might otherwise miss. Perhaps we could consider patience as suffering through someone else's shortcomings for a long period of time. It does not just happen once and it is over. It can take a long time.

"Accept one another, then, just as Christ accepted you..." (Romans 15:7). That verse makes me uneasy. "...just as Christ accepted you." Surely, Lord, you cannot possibly mean *just* as You accepted me? Unconditionally? Freely? No strings attached? You want me to accept others that same way?

"And we urge you, brothers, warn those who are idle, encourage the timid, help the weak, *be patient with everyone*" (1 Thessalonians 5:14). God, can we talk about this? How about if I am patient with most people? Everyone?! Be reasonable.

"*Love is patient...*" (1 Corinthians 13:4).

A major part of walking in true unity is being patient (suffering long) with others. ❖

Chapter 16

Maintain Loyalty to One Another

Recently I felt that the Lord was prompting me to study the life and actions of Moses. As I began to do this I realized more deeply than ever before some of the amazing things God had built within this man. His relationship with the Lord, his faith and his perseverance were all very evident. Yet, in the midst of all of these great attributes, I noticed one thing even more than anything else — his loyalty to his people.

In the midst of the attempts to convince Pharaoh to let God's people go, the Israelites were forced to do more work than ever. The extra work was brought on by Moses' efforts. When this happened his own people turned against him. "...and they said, 'May the Lord look upon you and judge you! You have made us a stench to Pharaoh and his officials and have put a sword in their hand to kill us'" (Exodus 5:21).

What would you have done in this situation? Our reaction today would be something like, "I am certainly not going to continue to try to help those ungrateful wretches." However, even though the people were vehemently opposing him, Moses continued to be loyal to them. At a time when most men would have given up and walked away, Moses continued on.

Later, Moses' obvious care for and loyalty to the people shines through even more brightly. At the request of the people, Aaron made a golden calf for them to worship. God became very angry with the people and threatened to annihilate them and replace them with a nation from Moses' seed (Exodus 32:10). Moses' response is almost unbelievable: "Why should the Egyptians say, 'It was with evil intent that He brought them out, to kill them in the mountains and to wipe them off the face of the earth'? Turn from Your fierce anger; relent and do not bring disaster on Your people" (Exodus 32:12).

When I read stories of God's dealings with people in the Bible, I often try to imagine myself in their place. I consider what I might do in the same situation. In this case I am convinced that my response would have been quite different from Moses'. I probably would have thought how nice it would be to have my own nation. It would be wonderful to have people throughout history referring to *my* God as *the* God. After all, I would have rationalized, the people were guilty. God had every right to destroy them. They had seen His sovereign power lead them out of Egypt and sustain them until this time, and yet they suddenly decided they needed another god. The Lord could have wiped them from the face of the earth and been completely justified in doing it.

Fortunately, Moses' thinking was much different from mine. Even though the people were completely wrong, he chose to stand with his people, upholding them. Given the same situation, what would be your reaction?

Moses' Loyalty — Too Good to Be True

Moses' loyalty to such fickle people was almost too good to be true. Later in the same chapter Moses was again speaking with the Lord. He said, "Oh, what a great sin these people have committed! They have made themselves gods of gold. But now, please forgive their sin — but if not, then blot me out of the book You have written" (Exodus 32:31). Moses is saying to God, "If You destroy this people then You'll have to destroy me too!"

Please understand that Moses was completely innocent in this situation. He was not only not involved, he was up on the mountain when the sin was committed. He was free and clear in the sight of God. Yet he chose to side with his brethren. He chose to stand in the gap on behalf of his people.

Our normal thinking today is much like what I thought when I put myself in Moses' place. We tend to dwell on the fact of the guilt (or difference of opinion, misunderstanding, etc.) instead of on the realization that we are brothers. The Lord places a high priority on our care for one another. "How good and pleasant it is when brothers live together in unity! It is like precious oil poured on the head, running down on the beard, running down on Aaron's beard, down upon the collar of his robes. It is as if the dew of Hermon were falling on Mount Zion. For there the Lord bestows His blessing, even life forevermore" (Psalm 133:1-3). God's best for us is that we remain loyal to one another in every situation.

The marvelous thing in this whole story of Moses is that God honored his stand. The Lord could have easily said, "Okay, if that's the way you want it, I'll destroy all of you and start over." But He did not. Instead, God honored Moses' loyalty to his brethren and ultimately withdrew His hand of judgement toward Israel.

God wants that kind of loyalty among His people. He's not interested in a half-hearted, I'll-be-loyal-when-it's-convenient attitude. The Lord wants our loyalty all the time.

True Loyalty

Some time ago I was teaching a worship seminar at a church. To stress a particular point, I shared a story about a husband who had left his wife. At the conclusion of the story I noticed the worship leader from the church was noticeably crying. I considered stopping to pray for her, but I did not believe that was the right thing to do at the time. Later, during a break, I asked her about the tears. She explained that a while back her husband had left her. Not only had he left her but he had left her for a woman who was her cousin and who was also the youth leader at the church. He and the worship leader had married early in life and he had become everything to her. When he left she was devastated. She was so badly wounded that there were times she did not show up for worship rehearsals. There were even times she was absent on Sunday mornings — even when she was scheduled to lead worship.

This same church has an administrator for their worship ministry. This frees the worship leader to do what she does best and not be bothered with the details of organization. When the above scenario was going on the administrator approached the other members of the worship ministry with a choice: "We can either ask her to leave the team and totally devastate her life or we can help her through. Which one do you want to do?" They chose to help her through.

So when she did not show up for rehearsals they went on without her. On Sunday mornings when she was supposed to lead and failed to appear, the administrator posed the challenge to the music team: "Okay folks, who's going to lead this morning?" In the midst of all this, they covered so well for her that, although the congregation was aware of her situation, they were completely oblivious to the depth of her struggle.

When the worship leader began to put her life back together she went to the music team and thanked them. "You'll never know what you did for me," she said. "You loved me when I was so unlovable. You helped me through the toughest time of my entire life. Thank you!"

Love never fails. This is the type of loyalty we need in the Body of Christ. ❖

Chapter 17

A Challenge

I believe that the Lord is issuing a challenge to His people today. Acceptance or rejection of the challenge will determine how far we, as the Body of Christ, will go in fulfilling all that God desires for us. The challenge is this: Endeavor to walk in unity in all situations. This means:

- praying for unity

- loving one another
- admitting our need for one another
- being willing to follow leadership
- giving up our opinions for the sake of unity
- building friendship relationships
- walking in forgiveness toward one another
- honoring one another
- believing the best about one another
- encouraging one another
- speaking well of one another
- being patient with one another
- maintaining loyalty to one another

This challenge covers the full gamut of our Christian relationships. It encompasses those with whom we walk regularly and those fellow Christians with whom we have major doctrinal disagreements. It calls for a dutiful resolution on the part of each believer as well as a willingness to be held accountable when we miss the mark. Maintaining unity must become a part of our character. It must become part of how we live. "...to be ready to do whatever is good, to slander no one, to be peaceable and considerate, and to show true humility toward all men" (Titus 3:1-2).

Will you join me in accepting the challenge? How far we go as the Body of Christ depends on how willing we are to do this. We must be willing to have the attitude of my friend who said, "Unless he tells me himself I will not believe it." If we are willing to take this stand, God will honor it just as He did with Moses. If we are willing to uphold our brethren, we will see unparalleled healing and forgiveness within the Church.

Let me offer one possible scenario of how this entire concept might play out in the course of human events. I am convinced that our nation is on the verge of spiritual, moral and economic collapse. It may not actually happen, but I believe we are teetering on the brink and it could go either way.

Some time ago I heard a story about a man who had made his fortune early in life and then lost it in the great depression. He later went on to become the head of a Fortune 500 company. One day someone asked him what the difference would be between a depression in the 1930's and a depression in the 1990's. His response was immediate. In essence he said, "That's easy. In the 1930's people were together. Families lived together. There was a sense of caring and community. That's not true in the 1990's. A depression in the 1990's would be far, far more devastating."

About a year ago I attended a missions conference and had the opportunity to hear a young lady who was born and raised in communist Russia. She had been brought up as a Christian, and, because of this, suffered much persecution. She told of being ridiculed by teachers in school and ostracized by fellow students. She shared many stories about rampant abuse and harassment they received simply because they were following the Savior. However, one of her statements stood out to me. She said that even in the midst of such persecution the Christians often suffered less than other people because they helped and cared for one another.

In the midst of my possible scenario of a 1990's depression (please understand that I am not predicting this, only offering it as one possibility), what would happen if there was a group of people in your community who cared for each other intensely? What if these people always said very positive things about each other? What if there was an obvious undying loyalty among these people? Do you suppose that such a people could impact your community for Jesus?

Remember, Jesus told us that the people of the world would know that we are His disciples because of our love for one another. He did not say that it would be because we all agreed on every doctrinal issue (or even on most of them). People will know because of our love for one another — a love which bears all things, believes all things, hopes all things, endures all things... a love which *never fails*. In every situation we must make it a priority to do the things that will bring about unity in the Church.

"...make my joy complete by being like-minded, having the same love, being one in spirit and purpose" (Philippians 2:2).

"Make every effort to keep the unity of the Spirit through the bond of peace" (Ephesians 4:3).

"May the God who gives endurance and encouragement give you a spirit of unity among yourselves as you follow Christ Jesus, so that with one heart and mouth you may glorify the God and Father of our Lord Jesus Christ" (Romans 15:5-6). ❖

Additional Scriptures for Further Study

He who loves a pure heart and whose speech is gracious will have the king for his friend. (Proverbs 22:11)

But I tell you that men will have to give account on the day of judgement for every careless word they have spoken. For by your words you will be acquitted, and by your words you will be condemned. (Matthew 12:36-37)

For if you forgive men when they sin against you, your heavenly Father will also forgive you. But if you do not forgive men their sins, your Father will not forgive your sins. (Matthew 6:14-15)

Therefore I tell you, whatever you ask for in prayer, believe that you have received it, and it will be yours. And when you stand praying, if you hold anything against anyone, forgive him, so that your Father in heaven may forgive you your sins. (Mark 11:24-25)

If your brother sins, rebuke him, and if he repents, forgive him. If he sins against you seven times in a day, and seven times comes back to you and says, 'I repent,' forgive him. (Luke 17:3-4)

We have different gifts, according to the grace given us. If a man's gift is prophesying, let him use it in proportion to his faith. If it is serving, let him serve; if it is teaching, let him teach; if it is encouraging, let him encourage; if it is contributing to the needs of others, let him give generously; if it is leadership, let him govern diligently; if it is showing mercy, let him do it cheerfully. (Romans 12:6-8)

Bibliography

1. Otis, George, Jr. *The Last of the Giants*. Tarrytown, NY: Chosen Books Publishing Co., Ltd./Fleming H. Revell, 1991.

2. ibid.

3. Lewis, C.S. *Prince Caspian*. New York, NY: Macmillan Publishing Company, 1951.

4. Christenson, Larry. *Back to Square One*. Minneapolis, MN: Bethany Publishing, 1979.

5. Heil, Dr. Robert. *Bible Newsletter*, Volume 20, Number 1. Columbus, OH. 1993.

6. Ironside, Harry A. *Notes on the Epistles to the Philippians*. Neptune, NJ: Loizeaux Brothers, 1922.

7. Vine, W.E. *Vine's Expository Dictionary of New Testament Words*. Iowa Falls, IA: Riverside Book and Bible House.

8. ibid.

9. Hansel, Tim. *You Gotta Keep Dancin'*. Elgin, IL: LifeJourney Books, 1985.

10. Arndt, Elise. *A Mother's Touch*. Wheaton, IL: SP Publications/Victor Books, 1983.

11. Myers, Bill. *The Portal*. Minneapolis, MN: Bethany House Publishers, 1991.

12. Blank, Joseph P., "The Miracle of May Lemke's Love," *Reader's Digest*, October, 1982.

13. Swindoll, Charles R. *Growing Strong in the Seasons of Life*. Portland, OR: Multnomah Press, 1983.

Here's what leaders across the nation are saying about the teaching ministry of Tom Kraeuter:

"Tom loves God and loves people. As a friend, as a brother, and as a pastor, I can honestly and enthusiastically endorse Tom Kraeuter and Training Resources."

Dr. Rick Painter, senior pastor,
Christ the King Church,
Phoenix, Arizona

"I heartily recommend your ministry to the entire Kingdom of God..."

Dr. Robert Stauffer, senior pastor,
The Tabernacle Evangelical
Presbyterian Church,
Youngstown, Ohio

"Reports have come in that indicate that there will be lasting results in our churches from Tom's teaching and ministry."

Linda Sue Greer, D.M.D.
Indiana District Assemblies
of God,
Indianapolis, Indiana

"Not only is Tom's doctrine sound and his theology uncomplicated, but his teaching is ripe with practical applications and insightful illustrations. When you combine that with Tom's easy manner and sense of humor, I can say that we were truly blessed. Jesus Christ was magnified in our midst."

Leslie H. Young, pastor
Living Word Fellowship,
Voluntown, Connecticut

"Tom's ability to relate to people who are at different spiritual levels, and be accepted by non-denominational and denominational people alike is a real blessing and quite remarkable."

Tom Griesmer,
Church of the Rock,
Open Bible Church,
Castle Rock, Colorado

"I would, without reservation, recommend Tom's ministry, and believe that you would agree that after spending any amount of time with him, that he loves the Lord and His church with all his heart."

Tom Bushey, senior pastor,
New Covenant Church,
Carthage, New York

"Tom Kraeuter is a gifted, called, anointed man of God. He lives what he teaches. He is a man of high integrity and deep devotion. You will not be disappointed in Tom's ministry..."

Craig Rench, senior pastor,
First Church of the Nazarene,
Medford, Oregon

"We highly recommend Tom Kraeuter to the body of Christ."

Bishop Paul A. Thomas,
senior pastor,
Victory Christian Center,
Greenville, North Carolina

How about your church?

All of these leaders (and numerous others) have had their churches impacted by the teaching ministry of Tom Kraeuter. If you have found this book to be worthwhile, consider having Tom come and share his teaching gift with your congregation. Your church will be challenged and encouraged to move on in their walk with God.

Tom Kraeuter has been teaching at churches across the nation for over ten years. He was formerly the managing editor of *Psalmist* magazine, has authored two previous books and his writings have appeared in such magazines as *Ministries Today, Worship Today,* and *Worship Leader.* Tom teaches full-time at seminars, conferences and retreats across the nation.

A gifted teacher, Tom mixes stories and humor with scriptural concepts to make the teaching life-related and practical. He is presently the minister of worship at Christian Outreach Church in Hillsboro, Missouri. He has served in this capacity for the past ten years fulfilling the call of God on his life to "equip the saints for the work of the ministry" (Ephesians 4:12).

Tom and his wife, Barbara, and their three children reside in Hillsboro, Missouri.

For more information on having Tom or another gifted Training Resources teacher minister at your church contact:
    Training Resources
    8929 Old LeMay Ferry Road
    Hillsboro, MO 63050
    (314) 789-4522

Training Resources Order Form

TITLE / DESCRIPTION	PRODUCT #	QTY	PRICE	TOTAL
			Subtotal	
			Shipping/Handling	
			TOTAL	

US/Canada, add 10% on $0-$50. Over $50, add $5.00 only. For foreign orders
(outside US/Can) add 40% to all orders for air shipment, 15% for surface shipment.

PAYMENT OPTIONS
(check one)

⌐ Enclosed is my check or money order for $_____ in US currency.
   (Make checks payable to Training Resources.)

⌐ Credit Card
   Please bill my: ⌐ | **MC** | ⌐ | **VISA** | Credit Card Expiration Date:_____

   Card# _____

   Cardholder's Signature _____

Name_____

Address_____

City_____State_____Zip_____Country_____

Mail to: Training Resources • 8929 Old LeMay Ferry Rd. • Hillsboro, MO 63050
Please include street address as UPS does not deliver to P.O. boxes.
Please allow 4 - 6 weeks for delivery.
☎ Telephone orders (charge cards only) call: (314) 789-4522, ☎
Monday through Friday, 8:30 - 4:30 CST.